FAST FOOD MANIAC

ALSO BY JON HEIN

Jump the Shark: When Good Things Go Bad

FAST
FOOD
MANIAC

From Arby's to White Castle, One Man's Supersized
Obsession with America's Favorite Food

JON HEIN

THREE RIVERS PRESS
NEW YORK

Library of Congress Cataloging-in-Publication Data
Hein, Jon.
Fast food maniac: From Arby's to White Castle, one man's supersized obsession with America's
favorite food / Jon Hein.—First edition.
1. Fast food restaurants—United States. I. Title.
TX945.3.H45 2016
647.95—dc23   2015011805

ISBN 978-0-553-41803-3
eBook ISBN 978-0-553-41804-0

Printed in the United States of America

Book design by Lee Fukui and Mauna Eichner
Photograph credits appear on page 274.
Cover design by Christopher Brand
Cover photography by Destination America / Robert Willis

10 9 8 7 6 5 4 3 2 1

First Edition

*This book is dedicated to anyone who has ever
flipped a burger, salted the fries, scooped some ice cream, or
worked in any capacity at a fast food place.*

*On behalf of all the customers who might not always be
in the best of moods when you encounter them,
I would like to say, from the bottom of my heart, thank you.*

CONTENTS

Introduction   1

What Is Fast Food?   4

The NATIONALS

A&W   9

Arby's   12

Arthur Treacher's   15

Baskin-Robbins   17

Ben & Jerry's   20

Blimpie   23

Bojangles'   26

Boston Market   29

Burger King   32

Checkers   34

Chick-fil-A   36

Chipotle   39

Church's   42

Cinnabon   45

Dairy Queen   47

Domino's   50

Dunkin' Donuts   53

Fatburger   56

Five Guys Burgers and Fries   59

Hardee's   62

Jack in the Box   65

KFC	68
Krispy Kreme	71
Little Caesars	74
Long John Silver's	77
McDonald's	80
Nathan's Famous	84
Panera Bread	87
Papa John's	90
Pizza Hut	92
Popeyes	94
Qdoba	97
Quiznos	100
Roy Rogers	103
Sbarro	106
Sonic	109
Starbucks	112
Steak 'n Shake	115
Subway	118
Taco Bell	121
Tim Hortons	124
Wendy's	127
White Castle	130

The REGIONALS

All American Drive-In	135
Braum's	138
Burgerville	140
Cafe Rio	143
Capriotti's	146
Carl's Jr.	149
Carvel	152

Culver's	155
Del Taco	157
Dick's Drive-In	160
Duchess	163
El Pollo Loco	166
Elevation Burger	169
In-N-Out Burger	172
Krazy Jim's Blimpy Burger	176
Krystal	179
Pink's	182
Primanti Brothers	185
Raising Cane's	188
Shake Shack	191
Skyline Chili	194
Taco Tico	196
The Varsity	199
Wahoo's Fish Taco	202
Whataburger	205
Wienerschnitzel	208

JON HEIN'S BEST FAST FOOD LISTS

Burgers	212
French Fries	214
Milkshakes	215
Beverages	217
Fried Chicken	218
Hot Dogs	220
Pizza	222
Sandwiches	223
Tacos	225

Burritos   226

Fish   228

Ice Cream   229

Pastries   231

Coffee   232

Biscuits   234

Chili   235

Ice   237

Straws   238

Secret Menus   240

Drive-Thrus   241

Mascots   243

Sweepstakes   245

Toy Collectibles   246

Logos   248

Uniforms   249

Slogans   251

Ad Campaigns   252

Top Five Overall   254

Tips and Tricks   256

Secret Menu Item Dossier   261

In Memoriam   270

Acknowledgments   272

Photo Credits   274

INTRODUCTION

My name is Jon Hein. I am a fast food maniac. And I am here to praise fast food, not to condemn it.

There are over 220,000 fast food restaurants in America. Annual fast food revenue now exceeds $200 BILLION. One in four American adults eat fast food every single day.

That's a lot of people . . . and a lot of food.

When you define Americana, fast food is probably not the first thing that comes to mind. But just like baseball or apple pie, this speedy cuisine runs deep within the lifeblood of this great country. From A&W to White Castle, there is a ton of history behind countless great franchises that have literally helped shape this nation. One of these restaurants is just around the corner, or over at the mall, or at the next exit on the interstate. It's easy to find fast food.

When you enter any fast food place, you know exactly why you're there . . . and it's not necessarily for nutrition. Obviously it's for the food, but more important, the *comfort* of that food. These pages provide an understanding of where that comfort comes from. Some of it is history. Some of it is culture. And it's available all across this great land of ours.

Fast food is not as simple as it appears to be. There are so many different types of restaurants, and just like gourmet burger places and Mexican grills, this number continues to grow by the day. We have the national giants and the regional greats. The up-and-comers and the oldies but goodies. I've profiled many of my favorites right here.

The combination of my expertise and road tales is more powerful than two all-beef patties, special sauce, lettuce, cheese, pickles, and onions on a sesame seed bun. I grew up in Pittsburgh with a backyard that bordered on a McDonald's and fell in love with fast food. My seventh-birthday party at Roy Rogers is one of my fondest memories, and cross-country trips exposed me to this type of cuisine on a national scale.

Attending college in the land of Domino's (Ann Arbor, Michigan) gave me some midwestern exposure, and touring the country in a comedy troupe after graduating led to gulping down a Dairy Queen Big Q at Mount Rushmore, hitting KFC for a bucket in Moscow, Idaho, and sampling a Pizza Hut buffet in Missouri. Moving to New York opened my eyes to a whole new set of regional restaurants to sample and drive-thrus to cruise. As the great Johnny Cash once sang, I've been everywhere, man.

When I order meals at my regular stops, I don't even speak to the cashier since they already know my order. I've been asked to join White Castle's Cravers Hall of Fame. I've judged hamburger contests for Wendy's. Every Fourth of July, you'll find me at Coney Island gasping in awe at Nathan's annual Hot Dog Eating Contest.

With so many fast food places out there, it is critical to be thoroughly informed of what your options are in each section of the country. Within these pages, I definitively list which fast food establishments make the best of everything, from fries and shakes to straws and collectibles. You'll know the right time to go inside for your food versus when to wait in line at the drive-thru. And you'll be armed with an exclusive dossier of secret menu items.

As host of *Fast Food Mania,* a TV show you can still catch on Destination America (one of the Discovery channels), I profiled quick-service restaurants from Maine to New Mexico. Talk about a dream job. I learned plenty on this well-traveled road, and what surprised me the most is what customers really wanted to talk about.

It wasn't about the food. It wasn't about the service. It was about life stories. I enjoyed learning which state Nathan's gets its potatoes from (Maine) to make those legendary fries, but the gentleman who has made an annual pilgrimage to this Coney Island hot dog stand since 1934 fascinated me. I've shared some of these tales along with my personal experiences to illustrate how a simple fast food franchise can create lifelong memories.

The book has been organized so you can use it as a guide. The 43 national chains I've written about are listed alphabetically, followed by 26 of my regional favorites. Why 69? Everyone loves that number, plus it leaves you wanting more, which is how it should always be with fast food.

My "Best Of" lists cover 28 different fast food categories, culminating with my Top Five Overall chains. I've created an exclusive dossier of Secret Menu Items listed alphabetically by restaurant, so you can be prepared and in-the-know when you decide to go off the board.

Think of this book as a Guide to Colleges, except I'll be profiling the best fast food restaurants in America—Dominos and Primanti Bros., for example, instead of Michigan and Penn State. I couldn't include every fast food place that's out there, and I apologize if your personal favorite didn't make the cut. I've written about the dining establishments I know firsthand from my extensive research and found to be the best.

Fast food has changed lives in more ways than one. Some restaurants are better than others (go check my "Best Of" lists), but I think they're all pretty great. Even Burger King. See you at the drive-thru!

Jon Hein
November 2015

WHAT IS FAST FOOD?

Now, before you start asking why I included Domino's but left out Waffle House, allow me to break down *my* definition of fast food for the purposes of this book.

Fast food restaurants, also known as quick service restaurants (or QSRs in the industry), all have specific characteristics.

Merriam-Webster defines fast food as "relating to, or specializing in food that can be prepared and served quickly."

That's a good start. But, as always, there are rules. And some exceptions.

So what are my Rules of Fast Food?

RULE 1: *No Table Service*

You won't find a waiter or waitress at any fast food joint. Table service defeats the purpose and is a big no-no. Except for Pizza Hut. First rule, first exception.

RULE 2: *Drive-Thru*

If the restaurant has a drive-thru, it qualifies as a fast food establishment. Period.

RULE 3: *Speed*

Fast-casual, the latest trendy word in this wonderful culture, qualifies as fast food because it's all about getting your meal to you as quickly as possible as it's created right in front of your eyes. This is known as the "Subway Rule" since the largest fast food chain in the world was one of the first to serve assembly-line style, and also qualifies all of those Mexican grill places that seem to be popping up everywhere.

RULE 4: *Chains*

Fast food restaurants are typically part of a chain or franchise operation, which is good news for those who travel the country. On the regional side of things, I've made some exceptions for places that should be chains, but for whatever reason operate as a solo location. I told you there would be exceptions (you're welcome, All American).

RULE 5: *Pizza*

This is tricky. Pizza Hut offers table service, but also delivers, has takeout, and does its best to get pies out quickly. Domino's, Little Caesars, and Papa John's all *feel and taste* like fast food even though they are technically delivery places. This type of pizza breaks the rules—and qualifies as fast food as far as I'm concerned.

RULE 6: *Dessert*

I could not write this book without including my favorite ice cream and frozen custard places. Some of these also offer food, but I won't touch those menus because I'm there for the dessert anyway.

RULE 7: *Coffee and Donuts*

I have also included coffee and donuts. Most of these fine establishments have drive-thrus and no waiters, so that's enough for me.

Now, you *still* might be wondering why I failed to include certain fast food establishments. The answer is simple—this is my book, and I'm offering my personal take on fast food. I have been to countless other places and heard about even more, but with apologies to Zaxby's, Firehouse Subs, and a variety of drive-thrus around the country, I'll catch you next time.

I did break one cardinal rule, though, and skipped breakfast. This book is all about lunch, dinner, late-night snacks, and desserts.

There's plenty to digest in these pages. If you're looking for breakfast, I promise to cover it in the next book.

The
NATIONALS

ALL AMERICAN FOOD®

		SPECIALTY ITEMS	SECRET MENU ITEMS
ESTABLISHED	1919	Root Beer	Firecracker Burger
FOUNDERS	Roy Allen & Frank Wright	Bacon Cheeseburger	Mozza Burger
GAME CHANGER	Root Beer	Papa Burger	
FIRST LOCATION	Lodi, California	Root Beer Float	
TOTAL LOCATIONS	Over 1,200	The Frosty Mug	
TRADEMARK	Root Beer		
MASCOT	Rooty the Great Root Bear	**SEASONAL SPECIALS**	
CURRENT SLOGAN	All American Food		**BEST**
CLASSIC SLOGAN	That Frosty Mug Taste	**MUST HAVE**	Beverages (1)—*Root Beer*
		Root Beer in a Frosty Mug	Milkshakes (2)—*Root Beer Float*
			Mascot (5)—*Rooty*

Welcome Home, Soldiers

On June 20, 1919, there was a citywide party in Lodi, California, to welcome home World War I heroes, and Roy W. Allen felt that hot night would be the right time to open a root beer stand. A little less than a century later, that very same brand of root beer is still satisfying thirsts, but not just in Lodi.

That's one big barrel of root beer.

Two years after his initial success, Allen partnered with former Lodi employee Frank Wright to expand into the larger city of Sacramento, and the duo took the initials from their last names to name their root beer stand "A&W." The name stuck. This Sacramento drive-in was the first-ever franchised fast food restaurant, and Allen continued to sell franchises to others as he built the A&W chain.

Franchising is just one of many A&W fast food firsts. The chain expanded into Canada in the early fifties, paving the way for international sales. In 1963 it introduced the first-ever bacon cheeseburger, paving the way for many a satisfied stomach.

In the 1970s there were more A&Ws than McDonald's, and the company started a beverage division enabling anyone to take home that frosty mug taste. And in 1974, Rooty the Great Root Bear was born with a frosty mug in hand. But the '70s proved to be tough going, and franchises couldn't keep up with the growth. A&W scaled back its restaurant business and operates approximately 1,200 locations today.

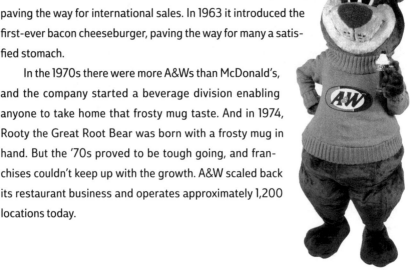

It's Rooty, always with a frosty mug in hand.

Fizz and Frost

A&W Root Beer's got that frosty mug taste!

The magic of A&W is, and always has been, its root beer, which is not surprisingly its best-selling item. A&W Root Beer has been prepared on-site at each location since day one, and there's nothing better than filling a frosty mug that was kept in the freezer just for you. Whether it's in a float or alone in your glass, you can always taste the freshness. I rank both beverages at the top of their respective classes.

Never underestimate the appeal of those frosty mugs. At an Ohio location in 1956, a happy couple met as they were swiping mugs from the restaurant. I kept one on hand in my freezer for years so I could re-create the effect with A&W from a can.

ESTABLISHED	1964	SPECIALTY ITEMS		SECRET MENU ITEMS	
FOUNDERS	Leroy & Forrest Raffel	Beef 'N Cheddar		Chicken Cordon Bleu	
GAME CHANGER	Quick Roast Beef	French Dip & Swiss		Sandwich	
FIRST LOCATION	Boardman, Ohio	Curly Fries		Meat Mountain	
		Jamocha Shakes		The Mike	
		Horsey Sauce		Wet Fries	
TOTAL LOCATIONS	Over 3,400				
TRADEMARK	Ten-Gallon Hat				
MASCOT		SEASONAL SPECIALS			
CURRENT SLOGAN	We Have The Meats	Arby's Melt		BEST	
		Arby-Q		Sandwiches (3)—*Roast*	
		Orange Cream Shake		*Beef Classic*	
CLASSIC SLOGAN	America's Roast Beef,	MUST HAVE			
	Yes Sir!	Roast Beef Classic			
		Curly Fries			

America's Roast Beef, Yes Sir!

Finding a fast food burger in the mid-1960s was never a problem, but grabbing a quick sandwich on the run was a different story. Leroy and Forrest Raffel saw an opportunity, and the brothers opened a sandwich shop in Boardman, Ohio, in 1964

The Roast Beef Classic

to serve hot, fresh roast beef to rival those quick burgers. They chose the name Arby's based on R.B., the initials of "Raffel Brothers" (and for their product of "Roast Beef").

The sandwich shop quickly became a hit, and the Raffels franchised Arby's restaurants across the country to those who shared their passion for hot, fresh roast beef. Arby's initially offered roast beef sandwiches, potato cakes, and soft drinks to customers. And you couldn't miss an Arby's driving down the street with its ten-gallon hat beckoning you to come in.

As Arby's grew and expanded its menu, it innovated products in various categories. The Beef 'N Cheddar became a staple with its classic Roast Beef sandwich. Curly fries had their own unique shape and proprietary seasoned batter on top, and don't forget the Horsey Sauce (a horseradish/mayo blend) for dipping. When it came to shakes, Baskin-Robbins was brought in to create a new flavor, the legendary Jamocha shake.

Customers appreciated these innovations and dedication to the quality of the food. Arby's became the first nationally franchised coast-to-coast sandwich chain and was ahead of its time. Arby's has been bought and sold a few times over the past few decades and its sandwich-making competition has grown tremendously. But if you're in the mood for a roast beef sandwich, just look for the cowboy hat and the curly fries.

Before Pharrell, there was Arby's.

They Have the Meats

It always feels comfortable walking into an Arby's, like it's a step up from rival fast food places. That's intentional, and the decor is designed to give customers a down-home feeling.

All fast food restaurants have a signature item, and for Arby's, it's the roast beef. The beef is sliced fresh in the store every single day, and you can taste that difference. The ultimate compliment is how most customers think of Arby's as just roast beef, but there's much more under its big hat.

Arby's side items are unique and well worth a taste. When I order my Meat Mountain or Big Montana, I can't wait for those curly fries (with Horsey Sauce, of course).

Arby's curly fries rival its roast beef.

I lost a lot of money betting that Arby's originally stood for "America's Roast Beef, Yes Sir," but the phrase was just a catchy advertising slogan. Now you can bet your friends and take their money as well.

ESTABLISHED	1969	SPECIALTY ITEMS	SECRET MENU ITEMS
FOUNDERS	S. Robert Davis, Dave Thomas, L.S Hartzog et al.	Fish 'n Chips Hush Puppies	
GAME CHANGER	The Perfect Butler		
FIRST LOCATION	Columbus, Ohio		
TOTAL LOCATIONS	Over 200		
TRADEMARK	Fish & Chips		
MASCOT	None	SEASONAL SPECIALS	
CURRENT SLOGAN	Treach Yourself		BEST
CLASSIC SLOGAN	Take Time Out for the Good Things In Life	MUST HAVE Fish & Chips Hush Puppies	Fish (1)

Supercalifragilisticexpialidocious

Arthur Treacher is a late English actor best known as the perfect butler from Shirley Temple films and as the legendary Constable in the Walt Disney classic *Mary Poppins*. So when National Food Corporation, led by Dave Thomas (yes, *that* Dave Thomas from Wendy's) and other fast food mavens, was looking for a spokesperson to bring fish and chips stateside, Mr. Treacher was the perfect Brit to underscore the character of the food. So perfect that they named an entire franchise after the actor. Now, *that's* a jolly holiday.

Fish and chips restaurants were opening all across America in the 1970s, and Arthur Treacher's became a fast food staple for many families. The flaky cod and thick fries provided an alternative to the plethora of burger and chicken joints that could be found on any corner. Eight hundred locations popped up in the United States, and although the menu was limited, the fish, chips, tartar sauce, and hush puppies were more than enough for everyone.

But there were rough seas ahead. The price of fish shot up, and suddenly these moneymaking fish and chips shops began to go under. On the strength of its brand name, Arthur Treacher's stayed afloat during some tough times and now is part of the Nathan's Famous family.

Fishy Fishy

Step in time with some flaky fish!

Arthur Treacher's was a personal favorite of mine growing up. I enjoyed Swanson fish and chips frozen dinners at home, so going to Arthur Treacher's felt like fine dining.

The crunchiness of the breading combined with the tenderness of the fish made for a scrumptious meal. The original fries were potato wedges, another detail that set this spread apart. Serving trays were outlined with faux British newsprint to create an authentic fish and chips feeling. I never felt like I was in England, but it did feel like a royal kind of meal.

ESTABLISHED	1945	SPECIALTY ITEMS	SECRET MENU ITEMS
FOUNDERS	Burt Baskin & Irv Robbins	Birthday Club	Donut Sundae
GAME CHANGER	31 Flavors	Pralines 'n Cream	
FIRST LOCATION	Glendale, California	Chocolate Chip	
TOTAL LOCATIONS	Nearly 7,300 worldwide	Rocky Road	
TRADEMARK	31derful flavors		
MASCOT	Pinky the Spoon	SEASONAL SPECIALS	
CURRENT SLOGAN	More Flavors. More Fun.	A New Flavor Every Month	BEST
			Ice Cream (2)
CLASSIC SLOGAN	31 Flavors of Fun	MUST HAVE	
		Chocolate Chip	
		Pralines 'n Cream	

We Sell Fun, Not Ice Cream

Baskin. Robbins. Two names that instantly bring a smile to your face. In 1945 brothers-in-law Burt Baskin and Irv Robbins wisely decided to merge their Glendale, California, ice cream parlors and gave birth to what was to become the world's largest chain of ice cream specialty stores. A variety of flavors has always made Baskin-Robbins unique. Sure, there's the standard vanilla, chocolate, and

31derfulness!

strawberry—but also Rocky Road, Pralines 'n Cream, and the best chocolate chip ice cream you'll ever devour.

When I was growing up it was always an adventure journeying to Baskin-Robbins, because a new flavor would be waiting when you arrived. Brand-new flavors rotated in and out with the classics, so the 31derful in-store choices always provided a monthly surprise, and as co-founder Irv Robbins insisted, the store was about fun first, ice cream second. The Birthday Club (of which I am a proud, long-standing member) rewards you with a free ice cream cone on your birthday.

Clever innovations have always kept Baskin-Robbins at the top of its industry. The miniature pink taste spoon, hand-packed quarts, the monthly flavor countdown, mixing and matching new flavors . . . it's a never-ending pursuit of providing the best ice cream experience.

On with the Countdown

I vividly remember the first time I entered a Baskin-Robbins in Squirrel Hill, Pennsylvania. I wondered what the heck that "31" meant, and once I found out, I was hooked. I immediately signed up for the Birthday Club to guarantee a

Tell me this logo doesn't bring a smile to your face!

free cone every November 24. And an ice cream shop that had a new list each month ranking its flavors? I'm so there.

You see, it wasn't just the great chocolate chip ice cream that kept me coming back. It was its position on the monthly flavor chart. I could never understand how Gold Medal Ribbon or some other trendy flavor could grab the top spot, when steady favorites like mine and Rocky Road couldn't crack the Top Ten.

Another proud moment in my life was when I got my very own name tag working at a Baskin-Robbins location in Commack, New York. Having this job in high school enabled me to drive at night with my junior license. But the real appeal, of course, was all the chocolate chip ice cream I could stick that little pink flavor spoon into. I had my fair share, but I also got to learn how the ice cream was made and stored, and witnessed all of the smiles it brought to customers (except for my friends who wanted in on the free scoops).

Happy birthday to you!

ESTABLISHED	1978	SPECIALTY ITEMS	SECRET MENU ITEMS
FOUNDERS	Ben Cohen & Jerry Greenfield	Cherry Garcia	
		Chocolate Chip Cookie Dough	
GAME CHANGER	Chunks in the Ice Cream	Chunky Monkey	
FIRST LOCATION	Burlington, Vermont	Phish Food	
TOTAL LOCATIONS	Over 580 Scoop Shops	Chocolate Fudge Brownie	
TRADEMARK	Font & Flavors	Half Baked	
MASCOT	Vermont Cows	**SEASONAL SPECIALS**	
CURRENT SLOGAN	Vermont's Finest	Timely Pop Culture Flavors with a Sense of Humor	**BEST** Ice Cream (3)
CLASSIC SLOGAN	Vermont's Finest	**MUST HAVE** Chocolate Fudge Brownie	

A Five-Dollar Investment

Childhood friends Ben Cohen and Jerry Greenfield completed an ice-cream-making correspondence course from Penn State's Creamery (which is a must visit), relying on "mouth feel" to create unique flavors. The next year, the partners opened an ice cream parlor in a renovated gas station in Burlington, Vermont, and embarked on their quest to change ice cream, and the world, forever. They succeeded.

Ben & Jerry's has always been about having a good time. From its annual free cone day (the second Tuesday in April) to building the world's largest sundae, or creating flavors like Wavy Gravy and Cherry Garcia, there has always been a creative spirit behind the chunky product. But that wouldn't mean a thing if the ice cream didn't taste fantastic—and it does. You will always find quality chunks in any scoop of Ben &

The first ice cream flavor named after a legendary Bay Area guitarist.

Jerry's ice cream, which makes you feel like you're getting more out of it. Couple the uniqueness of the ice cream with Woody Jackson's artwork, and Ben & Jerry's is a brand that cannot be missed.

Half Baked, Ben & Jerry's best-selling flavor, is a combination of two other best-selling flavors: Chocolate Chip Cookie Dough and Chocolate Fudge Brownie.

Ben & Jerry's took on ice cream giant Häagen-Dazs in the early 1980s when it started packing pints, and the two guys from Vermont prevailed. Earthiness oozes out of Ben & Jerry's, and the company puts its money where its mouth is helping noble causes all over the globe.

Honeymoon in Vermont

When I first started working in Manhattan in my early twenties, my schedule led to a necessary dietary staple for dinner—a pint of

Ben & Jerry's Chocolate Fudge Brownie. (Free tip—put your pint in the microwave for 16 seconds; you'll thank my wife, Debbie, for that gem.) A few years later, I got married and decided to make a pilgrimage with my new bride . . . to Ben & Jerry's ice cream factory up in Vermont.

Almost twenty-five years later, we remember it as one of our favorite trips. Our journey was twofold: to find the original shop in Burlington and hit the factory tour in Waterbury (a required rite of ice cream passage).

Chocolate Fudge Brownie—tastes great live or in a pint at home.

As we drove through the picturesque Vermont landscape, I worried that our expectations might be set too high. We had our golden ticket—would there be Oompa-Loompas? Sadly there weren't, but we did learn firsthand how Ben & Jerry's makes its ice cream, and how they ecologically practice what they preach. I feel good supporting this kind of company, and Ben & Jerry's keeps creating unique flavors with plenty of chunks that handsomely support me.

Put down this book and go get a pint now . . . I'll be here when you get back. Grab one for me too!

ESTABLISHED	1964	SPECIALTY ITEMS	SECRET MENU ITEMS
FOUNDERS	Tony Conza, Peter DeCarlo,	BLIMPIE Best	The Blimpie Way
	Angelo Baldassare	Roast Beef and	Cheese Trio
GAME CHANGER	Big Subs from the Shore	Provolone	
FIRST LOCATION	Hoboken, New Jersey	Ham and Cheese	
		Blimpie Trio	
TOTAL LOCATIONS	Over 2,000		
TRADEMARK	Salad on a Sandwich		
MASCOT	Del E. Fresh	SEASONAL SPECIALS	
CURRENT SLOGAN	America's Sub Shop		BEST
CLASSIC SLOGAN	Simply Blimpie	MUST HAVE	Sandwiches (4)—
		Blimpie Best	BLIMPIE

Jersey Boys

Saint Peter's Prep buddies Tony Conza, Peter DeCarlo, and Angelo Baldassare knew they wanted to go into business together in Hoboken, New Jersey, during the mid-1960s. The trio heard about submarine sandwiches being sold down the shore, and after one visit they knew exactly what line of work they wanted to get into. They would bring this "salad on a sandwich"—aka meat but with a lot of vegetables— to North Jersey, but they didn't want to call them subs or hoagies. As they flipped

Jersey boys brought the sub north and called it a BLIMPIE.

through a dictionary, they noticed a blimp that resembled the large-size shape of their new sandwich, and the name Blimpie was born.

Blimpie franchises began to sprout up all over the country during the next few decades as demand for submarine sandwiches skyrocketed. Seeking further growth, Blimpie started to drift a bit from its core sub business as it expanded its menu, and Subway took advantage of this sudden shift and took off.

Keep in mind that this was all well before the salad and health craze that took over the country. Traditional favorites such as ham and cheese or a BLT are on the menu, but a BLIMPIE is what keeps customers coming back. This unique combination of fresh meat and vegetables would remain a staple for many years to come.

Blimpie has always been generous with its serving sizes.

It's a Bird, It's a Plane . . . It's a Blimpie

Blimpie offers a variety of different sandwiches, but the name of their famous sandwich is "BLIMPIE." A big Blimpie benefit is its generosity with the fresh-sliced deli meat, vegetables, and toppings. Peppers are a particular favorite.

Stop in the mall for some fresh meat.

There is also the option to build your own sandwich with quality ingredients at your fingertips. That means there is an endless "secret menu" of subs, I mean BLIMPIES, that you can create.

The Blimpie Way means that your meat is layered with lettuce, tomatoes, onions, oil, vinegar, and spices stacked between two slices of fresh Italian bread. The resulting sandwich actually resembles a big blimp, and when you're building a sandwich named after an enormous airship, I recommend going *Hindenburg*.

Famous Chicken 'n Biscuits

ESTABLISHED	1977	SPECIALTY ITEMS	SECRET MENU ITEMS
FOUNDERS	Jack Fulk & Richard Thomas	Buttermilk Biscuits	
		Cajun Filet Biscuit	
GAME CHANGER	Cajun Chicken	Sweet Tea	
		Dirty Rice	
FIRST LOCATION	Charlotte, North Carolina	Cajun Pintos	
TOTAL LOCATIONS	Over 600		
TRADEMARK	Made from Scratch Biscuits		
MASCOT	Bo	SEASONAL SPECIALS	BEST
CURRENT SLOGAN	It's Bo Time!	Fried Bologna Biscuit	Biscuits (1)
		Seasoned Fried Turkey	Fried Chicken (5)
CLASSIC SLOGAN	Gottawannaneedagettahava Bojangles'	MUST HAVE	Beverages (5)— *Legendary Iced Tea*
		Any Biscuit	
		Dirty Rice	

Spice Is Nice

It was 1977, the year of disco, bell-bottoms, and the debut of a fast food Cajun-style chicken restaurant in Charlotte, North Carolina. Jack Fulk and Richard Thomas had a spicy chicken recipe, fresh-made buttermilk biscuits, and a formula for success they called Bojangles'. Fast food chicken was everywhere, but Fulk and Thomas added the

Your friendly neighborhood Bojangles'.

Cajun spice that was missing. In just a few short years, no restaurant had a higher sales average than Bojangles' did as it began to expand in the United States.

The Cajun chicken and its spiciness is only part of why Bojangles' achieved such early success. The biscuits are what put this franchise over the top. It's hard to beat a freshly made buttermilk biscuit, and soon chicken was being stuffed inside of them to make a tasty sandwich. Bojangles' special spice was added to the Dirty Rice, Cajun Pintos, and other sides not previously available at fast food chicken restaurants. All of this spice gets washed down with some Legendary Iced Tea to complete the meal.

Bojangles' sticks to what works and rarely adds new items to its menu. The core menu is not much different from when Bojangles' opened back in the '70s. If it ain't broke, don't fix it—and that's a credo Bojangles' wisely continues to stick to.

Bojangles' chicken and biscuits deserve equal billing.

All About the Biscuit

The fast food fried chicken market is extremely competitive, and my biggest criticism of Bojangles' is a regional one. It seems to be part of the Confederacy, with only a handful of locations north of the Mason-Dixon Line. It's a shame, because its biscuits are the best in the business.

Yes, the biscuits are even better than the chicken, but that's not a knock on the franchise. Bojangles' is smart enough to give the biscuits equal billing on its menu, with varieties like the Cajun Filet Biscuit, gravy biscuit, and, of course, the plain biscuit. The consistency

Bojangles' plain biscuit.

of the biscuit is critical: It's soft but doesn't crumble at the touch. It's large but not overwhelming. And its texture feels as if it's been baking for hours destined solely for your mouth.

I hope Bojangles' will make its way north, since the War Between the States ended long ago. It will be welcomed with open arms and mouths. It's Bo Time!

ESTABLISHED	1985	SPECIALTY ITEMS	SECRET MENU ITEMS
FOUNDERS	Arthur Cores & Steven Kolow	Half Rotisserie Chicken Loaded Mashed Potatoes Macaroni and Cheese Creamed Spinach Sweet Corn	
GAME CHANGER	Rotisserie Chicken		
FIRST LOCATION	Newton, Massachusetts		
TOTAL LOCATIONS	Over 450		
TRADEMARK	Rotisserie Chicken		
MASCOT	Chicken	**SEASONAL SPECIALS**	
CURRENT SLOGAN	Time for Something Good	Thanksgiving Oven to Table Meal Tax Day Deal Chicken Meal	BEST
CLASSIC SLOGAN	Home Away from Home	**MUST HAVE** Rotisserie Chicken	

Before Market, There Was Chicken

There's nothing more comforting than a home-cooked meal, and in 1985 Arthur Cores and Steven Kolow wanted to bring comfort food to the fast food business. The Boston Chicken opened in Newtonville, Massachusetts, serving rotisserie chicken with a variety of delectable side dishes. As the aroma from the marinated chicken wafted to the streets, lines began to form out the door for some affordable, good-tasting comfort food—and the customers kept coming back.

The rotisserie aroma still brings customers inside.

Boston Chicken grew very quickly in the early 1990s and began to spread across the Northeast. The store stuck to its chicken and side dishes until the middle of the decade when it expanded the menu to turkey, meat loaf, ham, and sandwiches and changed its name to Boston Market. In 2000 McDonald's acquired Boston Market for its real estate, but decided to stick with the brand and help it expand. The chain was sold to its current owners in 2007, but the rotisseries never stopped spinning.

Making Your Own Comfort Food

The first time I entered Boston Chicken, I was impressed by a few things. There was a line, which meant demand was there. It smelled fresh and appetizing. I had been told the experience would feel like having a home-cooked meal, but I didn't have to wait in line at Mom's kitchen.

Once I spotted the cornbread, I knew I was in good shape. It's one of those unique sides that, if it's done right, keeps you coming back for more. Yeah, the

Building the perfect Boston Market beast.

chicken is delicious, but I love having the choice of fresh sides, from loaded mashed potatoes to simple steamed vegetables, as I build my own meal.

I'm a big fan of building my own fast food meals. Standard combo offerings are fine, but for me it's all about customizing. At Boston Market, I choose the amount of chicken and specific sides, but I'll mix things up to create a different experience every time. My one constant: the cornbread, also known as the anchor of my plate. Love that tasty square cube.

ESTABLISHED	1954	SPECIALTY ITEMS		SECRET MENU ITEMS	
FOUNDERS	David Edgerton &	The Whopper		BK BLT	
	James McLamore	Onion Rings		BK Ham and Cheese	
GAME CHANGER	The Whopper	BK Stacker		Frings	
FIRST LOCATION	Jacksonville, Florida	Big King		Quad Stacker	
TOTAL LOCATIONS	Over 13,000	Chicken Fries		Rodeo Burger	
TRADEMARK	The Whopper			Suicide Burger	
MASCOT	The King	SEASONAL SPECIALS			
CURRENT SLOGAN	Be Your Way	Summertime BBQ		BEST	
CLASSIC SLOGAN	Have It Your Way	MUST HAVE		Toy Collectibles (2)	
		The Paper Crown		Secret Menus (5)	

Home of the Whopper

Burger King has always been inspired by McDonald's. After visiting the McDonald brothers' original San Bernardino hamburger stand in the early 1950s, James McLamore knew he wanted to be in the burger business with his partner David Edgerton. The duo acquired a license to operate an Insta-Burger King franchise in Miami, and acquired the rights to the chain by the end of the decade.

McLamore and Edgerton were fast food innovators, creating the flame broiler that Burger King still prides itself on, the mascot Burger King in 1955, and its sig-

The Whopper

nature sandwich in 1957—the Whopper, which was created when McLamore noticed a rival's success with a larger burger and realized that size does matter. BK was soon acquired by Pillsbury and began to expand, powered by advertising like its "Have It Your Way" campaign in 1974.

The ability to customize a burger was welcomed with open arms as customers held the pickles and the lettuce. Burger King made an unsuccessful attack on its larger rival, McDonald's, by comparing burger size, and then embarked on many poorly received advertising campaigns, including Herb, Dan the Whopper Man, and BK Tee Vee. But this didn't stop BK from being the number two burger chain right after Ronald and crew.

Have It Your Way

Burger King has always played catch-up to McDonald's, a successful strategy for a number of years. When Chicken McNuggets entered the scene, BK followed with its own Chicken Tenders. Menu staples like the flame-broiled Whopper, the Original Chicken Sandwich, and having an option for onion rings instead of French fries helped to differentiate the two chains.

Rings—a unique, tasty BK offering.

I've never been a BK guy, which is strange because I'm all about having it my way. I respect the onion rings option, and Chicken Fries are a step in the right direction, but flame-broiling has never won me over. And I just can't stand that creepy King. I get trying to be edgy, but when you are scaring away your customer base, you might want to rethink your mascot.

		SPECIALTY ITEMS	SECRET MENU ITEMS
ESTABLISHED	1986	Big Buford	
FOUNDER	Jim Mattei	Baconzilla!	
GAME CHANGER	Double Drive-Thru	Fully Loaded Fries	
FIRST LOCATION	Mobile, Alabama	Banana Milkshake	
TOTAL LOCATIONS	Over 800 (with Rally's)	Wings	
TRADEMARK	Five Dollar Challenge		
MASCOT	Mr. Bag	SEASONAL SPECIALS	
CURRENT SLOGAN	It's in the Bag	Classic Shrimp	BEST
CLASSIC SLOGAN	Bag a Bigger Better Burger	MUST HAVE	
	Bargain	Big Buford	

Hamburger Nation

Cars and fast food have always gone hand in hand. In 1986 Jim Mattei took this popular combo to a new level with Checkers, which was all about neon, chrome, double drive-thrus, and fresh burgers. As Checkers gained popularity in the South, another chain called Rally's was having similar success in the Midwest, and in the late 1990s the two drive-thrus decided to merge.

With only a few tables out front, it's tough to find a seat at a Checkers drive-in, but you can always find good value. Checkers' credo is the five dollar challenge— when you walk into any fast food restaurant with five bucks in your pocket, how much food can you take home?

The double drive-thru, and lots of checkers.

Two Double Drive-Thrus Are Better Than One

I am admittedly lazy, but I've always been a fan of the drive-in or a drive-thru. Perhaps it's the *American Graffiti* in me, but there's something very cool about picking up a burger, fries, and shake in your car. The double drive-thru takes you back to a different time as you cruise through.

Checkers puts the "big" in Big Buford.

Checkers is about quantity and quality. The burger sizes are huge (think the Big Buford or Baconzilla!), the fry portions are always generous, and the shakes hit the spot. You might have to wait a little bit for your food, but who cares? You're in your car listening to some good music, and you never have to worry about finding a seat inside.

ESTABLISHED	1967	**SPECIALTY ITEMS**
FOUNDER	Truett Cathy	Chicken Sandwich
GAME CHANGER	Chicken Sandwich	Waffle Potato Fries
FIRST MALL LOCATION	Atlanta, Georgia	Icedream
		Freshly Squeezed Lemonade
TOTAL LOCATIONS	Over 1,900	
TRADEMARK	Two Crucial Dill Pickle Slices	
MASCOT	Cows	**SEASONAL SPECIALS**
CURRENT SLOGAN	Eat Mor Chikin	Peach Milkshake
		Peppermint Chocolate Chip Milkshake
CLASSIC SLOGAN	We Didn't Invent the Chicken, Just the Chicken Sandwich	**MUST HAVE**
		Chicken Sandwich
		Waffle Fries

SECRET MENU ITEMS
Blueberry Cheesecake Milkshake
Dog Treat
Free Icedream
Fried Chicken Club
Spicy Char

BEST
Sandwiches (1)—*Original Chicken Sandwich*
Fries (4)
Milkshakes (3)—*Chocolate*
Ice (3)
Drive-Thrus (2)
Logos (4)
Mascots (3)—*Cows*
Slogans (3)—*Eat Mor Chikin*
OVERALL (5)

The Cows Come Home

When Truett Cathy opened the Dwarf Grill in 1946, he kept two simple things in mind: focus on providing high-quality menu items and take very good care of your customers. In the early 1960s he invented the Original Chicken Sandwich, and with his commitment to quality and customer service in place, Chick-fil-A was born at the Greenbriar Mall in Atlanta, Georgia.

Behold the power of the Chick-fil-A Original Chicken Sandwich.

Chick-fil-A sprung up in malls all over the South serving that great chicken sandwich with impeccably polite customer service. In the mid-1980s the first freestanding Chick-fil-A restaurant opened, and additional items (waffle fries!) were added to the menu. Chick-fil-A slowly and steadily continued its growth, and in the mid-1990s cows started telling us to "eat mor chikin." The company continued to expand throughout the next decade and now has more than 1,900 locations in 42 states.

As Chick-fil-A continues to grow, its values remain the same. The restaurant

The Original Chicken Sandwich

remains closed on Sundays, and it often promotes from within—who better to open a new franchise than a former team member? And you will never find more polite fast food employees anywhere else. It's no wonder, given that several of Truett Cathy's grandchildren are now active in Chick-fil-A, and as the cows continue to promote the cause to eat more chicken, the company remains focused on serving the highest-quality menu items along with gracious customer service.

Eat Mor Chikin

I experienced the Chick-fil-A phenomenon firsthand at an opening in Greenville, South Carolina. I camped out with a bunch of other Chick-fil-A fans hoping to be one of the first 100 customers at the new franchise location. That would entitle me to free Chick-fil-A for one year. Dan Cathy, the president of Chick-fil-A, was there in his tent, as were a bunch of employees keeping everyone excited throughout the night. Early the next morning I got my free chicken pass, but I also had caught the spirit of Chick-fil-A.

This fast food franchise is doing things right. The chicken sandwich, waffle fries, and homespun milkshakes are delicious. The customer service is gracious and polite. You feel welcome at Chick-fil-A as if they are actually happy to see you stop by. Ask anyone at Chick-fil-A a question, and the response will always be, "My pleasure." Going that extra mile keeps me coming back for more.

The cows are always watching at Chick-fil-A.

CHIPOTLE
MEXICAN GRILL

		SPECIALTY ITEMS	SECRET MENU ITEMS
ESTABLISHED	1993	Burrito Bowl	NONE—But will
FOUNDER	Steve Ells	Soft Tacos	customize any order
GAME CHANGER	Earthy Mexican	Chips & Guac	(see page 263)
FIRST LOCATION	Denver, Colorado		
TOTAL LOCATIONS	More than 1,800		
TRADEMARK	Burrito Bowl		
MASCOT		**SEASONAL SPECIALS**	**BEST**
CURRENT SLOGAN	Food With Integrity		Burritos (2)
CLASSIC SLOGAN	Food With Integrity	**MUST HAVE**	Tacos (5)
		Chicken Fajita Burrito	Uniforms (2)
		Chips	

Food With Integrity

Steve Ells has always been about fine dining. After graduating from the Culinary Institute of America and cooking in an upscale San Francisco restaurant, he came to Colorado in the early 1990s to open his own fine dining establishment. To finance this dream, he opened a small Mexican restaurant in 1993 and called it Chipotle. This restaurant, located on Evans Avenue in Denver, is the smallest Chipotle in the world and has signatures all over its basement from those who have worked there.

This wasn't green chili and cheese—it was food with quality ingredients made with classic cooking techniques and served at a fast food pace. Steve quickly opened two other locations, and although he never intended for Chipotle to become a chain, he realized what he had going on in Colorado. His guiding principle was food with integrity, and what became the restaurant's eventual slogan was its recipe for success.

We built these tacos!

As the millennium approached, Chipotle continued to expand, beginning to serve Responsibly Raised meat in its stores. Chipotle committed to respecting the animals, the environment, and the farmers—and from its buildings to its barbacoa, everyone across the country ate it up. This philosophy doesn't stop at the ingredients—it translates into the building materials and packaging. Chipotle's kitchens have always been open, and as you go down the line you see your food being made with its fresh ingredients.

Chipotle now serves over 800,000 people per day from coast to coast. Burrito Bowls have overtaken traditional burritos recently, but the fine ingredients and classic cooking techniques remain the same. GMOs (genetically modified ingredients) are a thing of the past, and you cannot taste the difference. Ev-

More popular than a burrito.

erything is well thought out, from the bags with commissioned work from famous writers to the music, which is updated monthly at the restaurants. It's all about customers knowing where the food comes from and feeling good when they eat at Chipotle.

Tough to Say, Easy to Eat

I mispronounce *Chipotle* all the time. It's Chi-POAT-le, not Chi-POAL-te. I call it "Chip" to make things easier.

Chipotle is run like a well-oiled machine. When it's your turn, know what you want or immediately surrender and ask for help. Chipotle menus are simple—you build it and it comes. You need to stay engaged with your order as you make different choices down the line.

Every position in the restaurant is important, but in my opinion, the unsung hero at Chipotle is the linebacker. That's the person standing between the food assembly line and the chefs, making sure that your ingredients are

Chips & Guac—a Chipotle must.

fresh and ready to go. Next time you go to "Chip," just watch the line flow and see how smoothly things work. You'll appreciate that yummy burrito or bowl even more.

ESTABLISHED	1952	SPECIALTY ITEMS	SECRET MENU ITEMS
FOUNDER	George W. Church Sr.	Original Chicken	
GAME CHANGER	Jalapeño Peppers	Spicy Chicken	
		Double Chicken N	
FIRST LOCATION	San Antonio, Texas	Cheese	
TOTAL LOCATIONS	Over 1,650	Jalapeño Cheese	
TRADEMARK	Spicy Chicken	Bombers	
		Honey-Butter Biscuits	
MASCOT	Churchie	SEASONAL SPECIALS	
CURRENT SLOGAN	Have the Love	Big Tex Club	BEST
		Purple Pepper	Biscuits (5)
		Chicken & Waffle Bites	
CLASSIC SLOGAN	Kick the Bucket	MUST HAVE	
		Honey-Butter Biscuits	

Remember the Alamo

George W. Church Sr. was sixty-five years old when he decided to open a business selling carryout fried chicken in 1952. He opened his stand across the street from the Alamo in San Antonio, Texas, and called it Church's Fried Chicken to Go. It sold one product, fried chicken, and customers could watch their orders being prepared on the cookers. Three years later, jalapeños were the first side dish

Church's added (quickly followed by fries), and the spicy restaurant was a success. George passed away in 1956, but his son Bill picked up where Dad left off and began adding locations all around San Antonio. Bill and his older brother, Richard, developed a marinating formula that could be used anywhere, enabling Church's to bring its spicy taste outside of San Antonio.

The expansion plan in the mid-'60s was to open locations where the Colonel wasn't, and Church's became the first Texas-based fast food chain to go national. Church's wanted to catch up to Kentucky Fried Chicken and became the second-largest chain in the poultry game.

Old-school Church's—same great taste.

Church's decided to enter the burger market in the 1980s, mistakenly straying from the franchise's strength. An unfounded, outlandish rumor that Church's locations were owned by the Ku Klux Klan and served chicken that made African American males sterile hurt sales. Cajun competitor Popeyes leapfrogged Church's and eventually acquired the franchise, leaving a few hundred locations to spare.

The remaining Church's stores revitalized, adding menu items such as spicy chicken wings, macaroni and cheese, and collard greens. Church's was back and has continued to grow—good news for spicy chicken and jalapeño lovers across the country.

A Taste of Honey

When most folks travel to San Antonio, they're there to remember the Alamo. Not this guy—I wanted to honor the birthplace of Church's Chicken and enjoy some of my very own Texas spice. I wasn't disappointed.

A fried chicken franchise will only go as far as its herbs and spices will take it (just ask the Colonel). Church's serves 160 million handmade honey-butter biscuits

Honey-butter biscuits are a must.

each year—that's a lot of sweet bread. It took decades to find the right combination of honey-butter to complement the biscuits, and it was well worth the wait.

ESTABLISHED	1985	SPECIALTY ITEMS		SECRET MENU ITEMS
FOUNDERS	Rich & Greg Komen	Cinnabon Classic Roll		
GAME CHANGER	Makara Cinnamon	Minibon		
		Center of the Roll		
FIRST LOCATION	Seattle, Washington	Cinnabon Stix		
TOTAL LOCATIONS	Over 1,000	Caramel Pecanbon		
TRADEMARK	Classic Roll	Chillatta		
MASCOT	Mr. Bon (in Pakistan)	SEASONAL SPECIALS		
CURRENT SLOGAN	Life Needs Frosting	CinnaSweeties		BEST
CLASSIC SLOGAN	Ooey Gooey Good	MUST HAVE		Pastries (3)
		Cinnabon Classic Roll		

Rolling in Makara

It was 1985, and Rich and Greg Komen knew exactly what they wanted—the world's best cinnamon roll. They hired a local food connoisseur in Seattle and spent three months building something special. They traveled the world to find the right cinnamon, and ended up in Indonesia, where they found Makara. With only one item on the menu, the Komens opened Cinnabon at the SeaTac Mall. Soon airports and malls all over the country were luring in customers with that sweet cinnamon smell.

It is extremely rare when a single product can drive a franchise, but that's exactly what Cinnabon did. Cinnabon bakeries were soon opening all over the world, pri-

I'd love to swim in this Cinnabon sea.

marily in malls and airports. Cinnabon expanded its menu to include Mochalatta Chills to drink and CinnaPacks, ingenious prepackaged six-packs to bring home the "bon" for those on the go. Theme parks, casinos, train stations, military bases—if there were people gathered who could smell cinammon, Cinnabon would be there.

Oooh, That Smell

I confess to my complete inability to walk by any Cinnabon location without ducking inside and sniffing around. My favorite part when I give in and begin to chow down is the gooey frosting that's all over the roll. It's always the right amount of goo, enough to get all over my fingers, but not too much, which would cause it to drip all over the place.

Cinnabon frosting is comprised of many different ingredients, with one of its most tasty being cream cheese. Knowing all the ingredients is one thing—using them in the right proportions is where the magic happens. I don't think "goo" is offered on its own, but it should be. I'll take a jar to go. As the folks at Cinnabon like to say, life needs frosting.

ESTABLISHED	1940	SPECIALTY ITEMS		SECRET MENU ITEMS	
FOUNDER	John Fremont McCullough	Blizzard		Banana Split Blizzard	
GAME CHANGER	The Blizzard	Dilly Bar		Chocolate Chip Blizzard	
FIRST LOCATION	Joliet, Illinois	Dipped Cone		Jack and Jill	
TOTAL LOCATIONS	Over 6,500	Buster Bar			
TRADEMARK	The Curl on Top	Banana Split			
MASCOT	Mr. Curly Cone				
CURRENT SLOGAN	Fan Food Not Fast Food	SEASONAL SPECIALS			
		Blizzard of the Month		BEST	
		Frozen Hot Chocolate		Milkshakes (1)—*Blizzard*	
CLASSIC SLOGAN	We Treat You Right	MUST HAVE		Ice Cream (1)	
		Oreo Blizzard			
		Vanilla Cone			

Queen of Them All

In 1938 John Fremont McCullough and his son Bradley developed a formula for soft-serve ice cream. They tested it at a local ice cream shop and sold 1,600 servings in two hours. Two years later, McCullough named the shop Dairy Queen, since he viewed the cow as the queen of the dairy industry and soft serve the queen of dairy products. DQ had arrived.

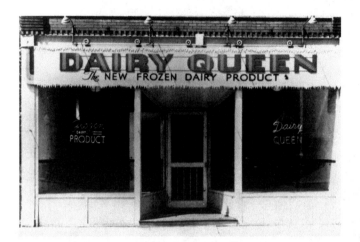

The very first DQ, in Joliet, Illinois.

Dairy Queen quickly franchised throughout the United States, serving vanilla cones with that signature curl on top. Some DQs still do not offer chocolate ice cream to this day.

That's me flipping my very own DQ Blizzard. A lifelong dream come true (and not one drop on the floor).

The 1950s ushered in the banana split and Dilly Bar. Fast food staples like burgers and fries were soon introduced, but let's face it, we were always there for the ice cream. Dairy Queen became a fixture of small-town America during the next two decades, and countless families have happy memories of their first trips to DQ.

Dairy Queen continued to expand, but in 1985 a franchisee came up with a game changer—the Blizzard. This best-selling concoction is so thick that you can flip it over without a drop of ice cream falling to the floor. More than 175 million Blizzards were sold in its first year. DQ has expanded (as have I) its food and ice cream menu over the years, but even with the success of the Blizzard it never abandoned the basics.

Warren Buffett Doesn't Miss

I love DQ. So does Warren Buffett (Dairy Queen is a wholly owned subsidiary of Berkshire Hathaway). Its secret is the temperature that the ice cream freezes at. Those exact degrees create the consistency that millions have fallen in love with. And that curl on top of the cone: think of a clock and move your hand 9–1–7. That's exactly how you make it— now all you need is a DQ ice cream dispenser.

I have never tried the food at Dairy Queen. It might be fantastic, but I am there for one reason, and one reason only: the ice cream. The best "shake" in the business arrived in the 1980s, and I've wholeheartedly supported it ever since.

Dairy Queen recently returned to my home of Long Island after being away for decades. My wife and I

Oreo Blizzard and vanilla cone—I could live on only this. I'm not joking.

visited the first week and waited for over an hour to get a local Oreo Blizzard. It didn't disappoint. It never does.

ESTABLISHED	1960	SPECIALTY ITEMS		SECRET MENU ITEMS
FOUNDERS	Tom & James Monaghan	Hand Tossed Pizza		
GAME CHANGER	Pizza Delivery	Pan Pizza		
FIRST LOCATION	Ypsilanti, Michigan	Thin Crust Pizza		
TOTAL LOCATIONS	Over 11,500	Cheesy Bread		
TRADEMARK	The Domino			
MASCOT	The Noid (old school)	SEASONAL SPECIALS		
CURRENT SLOGAN	Oh Yes We Did	Specialty Chicken		BEST
		Thanksgiving Feast		Pizza (1)
CLASSIC SLOGAN	You Got 30 Minutes	MUST HAVE		
		Original Cheese Pizza		

From DomiNick's to Domino's

In 1960 Tom Monaghan and his brother James bought DomiNick's, a pizza store in Ypsilanti, Michigan, for $900. This was the beginning of the world's largest pizza chain. The next year, James traded his half of the business to his brother for a Volkswagen Beetle, and Tom renamed the business Domino's Pizza. The dots in the logo were meant to geographically represent each Domino's location, but expansion prevented the logo from being updated after three stores. Imagine what a mess that logo would be today.

I put my money where my mouth is.

The key to Domino's success has always been speedy delivery. Domino's was built for franchising, and as time passed it quickly became the fastest-growing pizza place in the country. Its menu didn't change until 1989, when Domino's introduced a pan pizza, as it opened its 5,000th store.

Over the years, Domino's has continued to modify its menu by adding breadsticks, thin-crust pizza, chicken, sandwiches, and desserts. They might have dropped the "Pizza" from the name, but the core of the business remains the same—quick delivery of a pizza that's hot when it gets to your door.

Domino's in Ann Arbor

The dots represent the first three Domino's locations. I lived right by one of the dots.

Having attended the University of Michigan in Ann Arbor, the site of Domino's world headquarters, I became very familiar with Domino's Pizza my freshman year. I came from New York, where pizza has been perfected and there's an Original Ray's on every corner, and Domino's is not up to those standards. However, in a Michigan freshman dorm room, this cheese pizza hit the

Didn't have to leave the couch for this one.

spot in two ways—it was cheap and delivered to my door.

Domino's didn't offer the variety it currently does in its menu, but that didn't bother me at all. I would just order a second pizza (my metabolism was different then). Domino's guaranteed delivery in 30 minutes or less and always showed up on time.

Years later I was taking a carpool van to Detroit Metro Airport, and we had to pick up a passenger at Domino's Farms. I could not believe my eyes when I saw Domino's corporate headquarters, part of which I certainly helped build. It was tremendous, and I realized how all those inexpensive pizza orders can really add up.

ESTABLISHED	1950	SPECIALTY ITEMS		SECRET MENU ITEMS
FOUNDER	Bill Rosenberg	Glazed		Turbo Hot Coffee
GAME CHANGER	Donuts & Coffee	Dunkin' Munchkins		
FIRST LOCATION	Quincy, Massachusetts	Box O' Joe		
		Kreme		
TOTAL LOCATIONS	Over 11,300	Jelly		
TRADEMARK	Coffee			
MASCOT	Cuppy & Sprinkles	SEASONAL SPECIALS		
CURRENT SLOGAN	America Runs on Dunkin'	Heart Shaped Donut		BEST
		Pumpkin Coffee		Pastries (2)
CLASSIC SLOGAN	Time to Make the Donuts	MUST HAVE		Coffee (2)
		Vanilla Kreme		
		French Vanilla Coffee		

It's Worth the Trip

Bill Rosenberg knew workers needed two things hot and fresh in the morning—donuts and coffee. In 1948 he opened his first restaurant, Open Kettle, in Quincy, Massachusetts. Two years later, he changed the name of that location to Dunkin' Donuts and advised customers to dunk their donut in a ten-cent cup of coffee. DD was a hit and began franchising just a few years later. The variety of donuts kept people coming into the shops, but half of Dunkin' Donuts' sales were its coffee. Even

Protecting the original Quincy location. You'd better pronounce the town's name right.

today, Dunkin' Donuts uses the original propietary coffee blend recipe established by its founder.

In 1972 Dunkin' Donuts raised the stakes with a new item that looked like the punched-out center of the donut—a Munchkin. These tiny pastries were instantly popular and helped the chain further expand. Other pastries, breakfast sandwiches, and different flavors of coffee were added to the menu, but donuts and coffee remain the keys to Dunkin's success.

The 1980s ushered in Fred the Baker, who reminded us all when it was "time to make the Donuts." This legendary spokesman drowsily kept us hooked for almost fifteen years. Competitors have come and gone, but DD remains atop the donut and coffee sales category, and it won't slow down as long as America keeps runnin' on Dunkin'.

Now, THAT'S a good cup of coffee.

Time to Make the Donuts

The amount of donuts and coffee served by Dunkin' Donuts is truly staggering. More than 5 million customers stop in each day. Thirty cups of coffee are served per second. There are over 15,000 ways to order your coffee at Dunkin' Donuts, and French Vanilla is the most popular flavored coffee in the country.

But let's talk about the donuts. There are endless varieties available for your tasting. A box of Munchkins is a good way to sample flavors until you find your favorite. My quick half dozen is composed of the classic Glazed, Boston Kreme, Powdered Sugar, Vanilla Kreme Filled, Jelly, and Old Fashioned.

I got to play around at Dunkin' Donuts headquarters up in Massachusetts and actually make the donuts. Every batch is made with

In the Dunkin' corporate kitchen. Yum.

great care, and no new flavors are created without many mouthwatering trials and tribulations. They had to roll me out of that kitchen.

ESTABLISHED	1947	SPECIALTY ITEMS	SECRET MENU ITEMS
FOUNDER	Lovie Yancey	XXXL Fatburger	Hypocrite
GAME CHANGER	XXX Challenge	Homemade Onion Rings	
FIRST LOCATION	Los Angeles, California	Maui-Banana Shake	
TOTAL LOCATIONS	Over 150		
TRADEMARK	Custom Burgers		
MASCOT		SEASONAL SPECIALS	
CURRENT SLOGAN	The Last Great Hamburger Stand	Big Smoky BBQ Fatburger Strawnana Shake	BEST
CLASSIC SLOGAN	The Last Great Hamburger Stand	MUST HAVE XXXL Fatburger Onion Rings	

Lose the Mister

Lovie Yancey loved two things dearly—hamburgers and music. So she created a place in 1947 called Mr. Fatburger on Western Avenue in Los Angeles, where the burgers were big and the music played all night. Touring musicians would stop by

Now, that's a tasty burger.

during their L.A. gigs, and Lovie would have delicious homemade food waiting for them. In 1952 Lovie removed the Mr., and today's Fatburger was born.

Don't be fooled by the name. Fatburgers are huge and tasty, but they have always been made with lean beef. The onion rings are made from real onions. The shakes come from real hand-scooped ice cream. It takes a little bit longer to get the food, but once it comes you can really taste the difference. Fatburger remained mostly a California chain until the late 1990s, when it began to expand across North America.

King Me

Lovie Yancey made sure that great tunes accompanied her great food. And that spirit lives on at every Fatburger location, with custom playlists of the best music to chew to.

In fact, the franchise name became a go-to rap lyric around the turn of the century. Ice Cube, Tupac, The Notorious B.I.G., and the Beastie Boys included Fatburger in their lyrics, and a variety of hip-hop stars have opened Fatburger franchises.

I conquered the XXX Challenge.

As you're tapping your feet, if you're really feeling brave, you can take the Triple XXX Challenge like I did. Finish the two-pound triple-pattied burger with toppings, and get your picture on the wall. Pace yourself. There's a lot of meat to be had, and if you rush things, you won't be able to finish.

I was able to conquer this mighty burger challenge in Las Vegas, and pacing was the key. Slow and steady won the race. For the first time in a long time, I was a winner in Vegas.

FIVE GUYS
BURGERS and FRIES

		SPECIALTY ITEMS	SECRET MENU ITEMS
ESTABLISHED	1986	Hamburger	Cheese Fries
FOUNDER	Jerry Murrell	Cajun Style Fries	Double Grilled
GAME CHANGER	Fresh Burgers & Fries	Peanuts	Cheeseburger
FIRST LOCATION	Arlington, Virginia	Grilled Onions	Patty Melt
TOTAL LOCATIONS	Over 1,000		
TRADEMARK	5 Red Checkers		
MASCOT		**SEASONAL SPECIALS**	
CURRENT SLOGAN	Five Guys	Bacon Cheese Dog	**BEST**
CLASSIC SLOGAN	Five Guys Burgers and	**MUST HAVE**	Burgers (2)—*Hamburger*
	Fries	Hamburger	Fries (5)
		Five Guys Style Fries	

Go to College or Start a Business

Jerry and Janie Murrell gave the four Murrell sons an option—go to college or start a business. Lucky for us, they chose the latter and in 1986 created Five Guys Burgers and Fries in Arlington, Virginia. The Murrells took the money set aside for college tuition and sank it into the burger business. They needed a name, so Jerry thought about it, realized he had four sons, and did some quick math—Five Guys. In fact, the five red checkers on the wall in every location represent the five Murrell men. Only hand-formed grilled burgers and fresh-cut fries cooked in peanut oil would be served, and Five Guys quickly developed a cult-like following and became the best-tasting burger in the Washington, D.C., area.

Four local restaurants were soon added, and in 2003 Five Guys decided to franchise. Units have been sprouting up all over the country as their cultlike status continues to grow. Five Guys has always stuck to its principles, keeping its menu simple and fresh. When two customers enter, you'll hear a shout of "Two in the door" so the staff can be adequately prepared.

Note the red five-checker pattern and the smiling customer.

A Five Guys burger starts with two beef patties, and there are countless FREE toppings to be had if you so desire. There are over 250,000 ways to order a burger

The standard Five Guys burger features TWO patties—as it should be.

at Five Guys. The size of the fries is plentiful, and you have an option for Cajun Style or good old-fashioned Five Guys Style. As a bonus, an order of fries is topped off with an additional pouring of fries. Nothing here is ever frozen, and if you want to know where your potatoes hail from, the city name is on a black-board surrounded by plentiful free peanuts.

Delivery and Shakes

Five Guys doesn't compromise for anyone, including the president of the United States. When the commander in chief ordered some burgers and fries, Five Guys' "no delivery" policy remained intact. The White House dispatched personnel to pick up the president's order. You have to respect that.

The only thing missing at Five Guys is shakes; if the gang in red can't do something right, they won't do it at all. But they've been doing some regional testing (flavors include Bacon and Oreo!), so hopefully these guys will figure out how to keep ice cream as fresh as potatoes and burger patties.

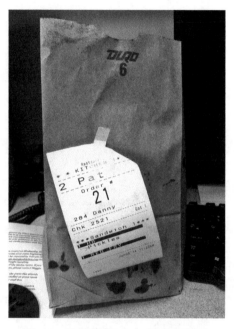

Grease spots on the bag—always a good sign.

ESTABLISHED	1960	SPECIALTY ITEMS	SECRET MENU ITEMS
FOUNDER	Wilber Hardee	Monster Thickburger	The Harold
GAME CHANGER	Huskee Burger	Six Dollar Thickburger	
FIRST LOCATION	Greenville, North Carolina	Crispy Curls	
TOTAL LOCATIONS	Over 1,900	Onion Rings	
TRADEMARK	Thickburger	Biscuit 'N' Gravy	
MASCOT	The Hardee's Star	**SEASONAL SPECIALS**	**BEST**
CURRENT SLOGAN	Eat Like You Mean It	Memphis BBQ	Biscuits (3)
		Thickburger	Straws (5)
		Bacon Cheddar Fries	Toy Collectibles (3)
CLASSIC SLOGAN	Home of the Huskee	**MUST HAVE**	
		Thickburger	
		Biscuit	

Charco-Broiled Goodness

Wilber Hardee opened the first restaurant of his namesake in Greenville, North Carolina, in 1960. From the get-go Hardee's would pride itself on its distinctive burger options, and the charco-broiled Huskee was a big hit. Many original Hardee's locations were built in the shape of a hexagon with a pointed roof. Even the burgers had a hexagonal shape early on—anything to distinguish the brand from

The hexagon is gone but the taste lives on.

other burger rivals. By the end of the decade, there were over 200 Hardee's locations satisfying hungry customers.

The 1970s ushered in more burger options, including the Huskee Jr., Big Twin, and Big Deluxe. If you were looking for a big burger, Hardee's was the place to go. Hardee's also introduced its Made from Scratch Biscuits, a big hit that remains a mainstay on the menu to this day.

Hardee's tremendous expansion was halted by the buyouts of the 1980s, and to save costs the new ownership changed the burger recipe and discontinued cost-lier burger options—including the elimination of Wilber Hardee's charco-broiling system. Hardee's tried to compete with Kentucky Fried Chicken and Arby's without the trademark technique that set them apart, but they came up short.

What's inside that box makes that star smile.

Hardee's has since been acquired by Carl's Jr. and is on the rebound since it got back to its charbroiling roots and being all about big burgers.

Big Big Burgers

The first time I went to Hardee's as a kid, I was immediately struck by the hexagon shape of everything. I wasn't sure if the burger was going to be good, but I did know that I was in for a unique fast food experience. I remember gawking at the size of the burger.

The Monster Thickburger

The appeal of Hardee's has always been how it embraces the size of a burger. It offers ¼ pound, ⅓ pound, ½ pound sizes, and doesn't shy away from loading up. The Monster Thickburger isn't just huge in name only—it's a sizable burger known as "audacity on a bun." Fast food gives you options, and Hardee's is the choice when you want to go all in.

On another trip to Hardee's, I decided to order only the biscuits. The plain Made from Scratch Biscuit is THAT good. It reminds me of the old Kentucky Fried Chicken biscuits before they switched their recipe. In my opinion, it is more than okay to fill up on bread at Hardee's.

in the box®

ESTABLISHED	1951	SPECIALTY ITEMS	SECRET MENU ITEMS
FOUNDER	Robert O. Peterson	Jumbo Jack	Additional Ingredients
GAME CHANGER	Drive-thru intercom	Ultimate Cheeseburger	Ciabatta Bacon
FIRST LOCATION	San Diego, California	2 Tacos	Cheeseburger
TOTAL LOCATIONS	Over 2,200		Sourdough Buns
TRADEMARK	Jack		
MASCOT	Jack Box	SEASONAL SPECIALS	
CURRENT SLOGAN	More Than 60 Years	Egg Nog Shake	BEST
	of Awesome	Bonus Jack	Ads (2)
		All-American Jack	Tacos (4)
CLASSIC SLOGAN	Jack's Back	MUST HAVE	
		Jumbo Jack	
		2 Tacos	

Hit the Road, Jack

In 1951 Robert O. Peterson opened a California roadside burger place to serve customers in their cars and called it Jack in the Box. The game-changing difference was its two-way intercom system and drive-thru window used to order your 18-cent burgers. The intercom system was concealed in the colorful collar of a clown perched atop the drive-thru menu.

The original Jack in the Box in San Diego, California.

Jack in the Box quickly expanded in the Southwest, equipped with the fastest way to get customers in and out of fast food restaurants. The company was acquired by Ralston Purina in 1968, which further expanded Jack in the Box during its fifteen-year ownership of the brand, but the restaurant began to resemble its competitors and lost its distinctiveness.

The speakerbox clown was ceremoniously blown up in a 1980 ad campaign that sought to differentiate the brand from other chains by highlighting premium items. In the mid-1990s, thanks to the miracle of plastic surgery, the mascot Jack Box returned as the company's fictional CEO, and the "Jack's Back" campaign is the longest ongoing advertising campaign in the fast food industry.

Jack in the Box's best-selling item—tacos.

Jack in the Box is now located in 21 states mostly in the Southwest, and fans love its advertising and tacos. The 2-for-99-cents tacos are the company's biggest seller! Jack's menu offers something for everyone, and his presence remains very much a part of the guest experience.

Jack's Back

When Jack in the Box came east, you couldn't help but notice it, thanks to its distinctive mascot. Along with the creepy King at BK, Ping-Pong-faced Jack also freaked me out. That smiling clown kept me away for a long, long time. Once I overcame my irrational fear, I got to enjoy the food inside and wondered what else I'd missed out on due to my trepidation.

I give a lot of credit to Jack in the Box for re-embracing Jack and making the most of him. It is a mistake to blow up the most distinctive feature of your brand, and the ad campaign that brought Jack back has worked incredibly well. Never underestimate the power of advertising when it comes to fast food. It can make or break your brand.

Classic Jack antenna ball.

ESTABLISHED	1930	SPECIALTY ITEMS		SECRET MENU ITEMS
FOUNDER	Colonel Harland Sanders	Original Recipe		Mac and Cheese Bowl
GAME CHANGER	Pressure Cooker	Extra Crispy		Poutine
FIRST LOCATION	Corbin, Kentucky	Biscuits		Side of Biscuits
		Mashed Potatoes		Triple Down
TOTAL LOCATIONS	Over 18,000			BEST
TRADEMARK	The Colonel			Fried Chicken (1)—
MASCOT	The Colonel	SEASONAL SPECIALS		*Original Recipe*
CURRENT SLOGAN	Finger Lickin' Good	Festive Feast		Biscuits (4)
		Chicken Littles		Slogans (4)—*It's Finger*
				Lickin' Good
CLASSIC SLOGAN	It's Finger Lickin' Good	MUST HAVE		Sweepstakes (3)
		Original Recipe		Mascots (2)—*The*
		Biscuit		*Colonel*

The Colonel

In 1930, forty-year-old Harland Sanders was operating a gas station in Corbin, Kentucky, and cooked for weary travelers who stopped to fill their tanks. There was no restaurant, so customers ate at a table inside the service station. But soon people would show up for just the chicken and not the gas. The governor of Kentucky even

The Colonel and his bucket.

made Sanders a colonel for his contribution to the state's cuisine back then. The Colonel perfected his blend of 11 herbs and spices and the cooking technique that is still used today at KFC. An interstate rerouted the car traffic, but people still found their way to Corbin to sample the chicken at the Sanders Café.

Twenty-five years after his initial success, the Colonel decided to bring his Kentucky Fried Chicken outside of the state, and franchises began popping up all throughout the United States, the first being in Utah. Colonel Sanders was sixty-five years old and arguably becoming the world's most famous cook. Chicken was a rival to the dominant hamburger fast food places, thanks to Colonel Sanders.

Kentucky Fried Chicken was served in a paper bucket featuring a picture of the Colonel and a reminder that it's finger lickin' good. Sanders sold the company but will always be the face of the franchise. In the early 1990s the name was changed to KFC (for signage reasons and to downplay the "fried"), and its menu expanded to sandwiches, wings, and other sides.

Hot or Cold

I am an unabashed lifelong fan of Kentucky Fried Chicken. The most fascinating aspect of the chicken is that it tastes just as good *cold* as

KFC warm and fresh biscuits.

it does *warm*. If you don't fill up at first, throw it in the fridge and eat your chicken cold later.

At KFC headquarters outside of Louisville, Kentucky, I was shown the safe where the original recipe is kept, and the 11 herbs and spices remain a locked-down secret to this day. If I only had that combination. I pondered this at the Colonel Sanders Museum located right next door and realized how far great-tasting chicken can take you.

I highly recommmend making the pilgrimage to Corbin, Kentucky. The original location has been preserved with the Colonel's kitchen intact for you to peruse. It's not

The kitchen where the Colonel blended his 11 herbs and spices.

hard to imagine traffic rolling through town before the interstate was built and stopping by for some of Colonel Sanders's freshly made chicken.

I do miss the traditional bucket. This chicken container was so popular that many locations built them onto their signs out front. The original bucket meal of 14 pieces of chicken, 5 rolls, and a pint of gravy filled up families for years. They can change the name, but it will never be KFC for me . . . it will always be Kentucky Fried Chicken.

		SPECIALTY ITEMS	SECRET MENU ITEMS
ESTABLISHED	1937	Original Glazed	Cup of Glaze
FOUNDER	Vernon Rudolph	Glazed Doughnut Holes	Filled Doughnut Holes
GAME CHANGER	Original Glazed	Traditional Cake	Free Doughnut
FIRST LOCATION	Winston-Salem, North Carolina	Chocolate Iced with KREME Filling	
TOTAL LOCATIONS	Over 1,000		
TRADEMARK	HOT NOW sign		
MASCOT		**SEASONAL SPECIALS**	
CURRENT SLOGAN	Doughnuts and Coffee Since 1937	Caramel Dutch Apple Pie	**BEST**
		Key Lime Pie	Pastries (1)
CLASSIC SLOGAN		**MUST HAVE**	Coffee (5)
		HOT Original Glazed	Logos (2)

What's That Smell?

Vernon Rudolph bought a secret doughnut recipe from a New Orleans French chef in 1937 and began baking these pastries in Winston-Salem, North Carolina, naming them Krispy Kreme. The scent from baking the doughnuts drifted onto the street, and people were interested in buying them on the spot. So Vernon cut a hole in an outside wall and sold hot doughnuts directly to customers on the sidewalk. From that

A Krispy Kreme factory with an entrance for customers to buy hot doughnuts before delivery.

day forward, customers could see exactly how Krispy Kreme doughnuts get made and have the opportunity to eat them hot and fresh.

Krispy Kreme created their celebrated doughnuts to be delivered to locations all across the region. It wasn't until the 1980s that stores exclusively for retail sales were opened. These stores captured the magic of the factories by keeping the entire doughnut-making process visible to the customer. There wasn't just a pretty display case to see—the entire trip of the doughnut was there for you to behold as the smell of hot doughnuts wafted through the shop.

In 1992 the HOT NOW sign was created to indicate when a fresh batch of doughnuts is coming fresh off the line. This beacon brings countless drivers into the store for a hot doughnut and coffee (and now there's an app for that). The Original Glazed doughnut remains a favorite, and shaped doughnuts and other variations have become part of all that Krispy Kreme has to offer.

As the source of the best-tasting doughnuts rapidly expanded across the land, Krispy Kreme had some accounting issues that led to shutting down many of its retail stores. Krispy Kreme doughnuts, however, are still made fresh daily and delivered to countless markets, stores, and other places throughout the country.

The traffic-stopping HOT NOW sign.

Glazed Magic

If you want to view paradise, simply look around a Krispy Kreme store. If I'm on the road and see a HOT NOW sign lit up, I immediately make a turn for Krispy Kreme. There's a Wonka-like feeling when you enter, as doughnuts are created right in front of your eyes. Pick up your baker's hat and watch your doughnut take a magical journey

What I wouldn't give to be a Krispy Kreme doughnut.

under the glazed fountain, eventually ending up in your mouth.

Krispy Kreme affects all of your senses, and of course you can't eat just one doughnut. The Original Glazed is so light and can be devoured in seconds, and when it's hot it is simply magical.

One day, when I open the Krispy Kreme theme park, there will be a ride where you sit in a round doughnut and float under a cascading fountain of glaze. Added bonus—you get to eat your float, but only at the end of the ride.

Little Caesars

ESTABLISHED	1959	**SPECIALTY ITEMS**		**SECRET MENU ITEMS**	
FOUNDERS	Mike & Marian Ilitch	HOT-N-READY Classic		Half and Half Pizza	
GAME CHANGER	Pizza!Pizza!	Cheese		No Cheese Pizza	
FIRST LOCATION	Garden City, Michigan	DEEP!DEEP! Dish		Stuffed Crust Pizza	
TOTAL LOCATIONS	About 4,000	Crazy Bread			
TRADEMARK	Pizza!Pizza!				
MASCOT	Little Caesar	**SEASONAL SPECIALS**			
CURRENT SLOGAN	Pizza!Pizza!			**BEST**	
CLASSIC SLOGAN	Pizza!Pizza!	**MUST HAVE**		Pizza (3)	
		Crazy Bread		Mascots (4)—*Little*	
		Pizza!Pizza!		*Caesar*	

All Hail Caesar

Mike and Marian Ilitch used $10,000 in life savings to open a carryout pizza restaurant at a strip mall in Garden City, Michigan, in 1959. Marian considered Mike to be her "little Caesar," and this original location (which is still open today) was christened "Little Caesar's Pizza Treat." This store's success quickly led to other franchises and a shortened name—Little Caesars. By 1987 Little Caesars was in all fifty states, a national pizza chain.

The first Little Caesar's, which is still open today.

Little Caesars has always been an innovator in the pizza industry. Many were skeptical of a carryout restaurant without tables and chairs, but they were proven wrong. Little Caesars' most famous idea was offering two pizzas for the price of one, which would come to be known as Pizza!Pizza! A conveyor oven was specifically designed to bake pizza quickly and keep up with demand. Pizza by the Foot and Pan!Pan! pizzas were other unique offerings. Yet another innovation, Crazy Bread, became the ultimate pizza side dish and was copied by competitors.

Great pizza at a great price has helped Mike Ilitch become the owner of the Detroit Red Wings and the Detroit Tigers—that's a lot of Pizza!Pizza! Adding carryout pizza has helped make Little Caesars the fastest-growing pizza chain in the world.

Love this guy. Pizza!Pizza!

Pizza!Pizza!

I sampled Little Caesars for the first time when I was a student at the University of Michigan. The idea of two pizzas for the price of one appeals to any student looking to not spend a lot of money. What I didn't expect, though, was the ultimate pizza delivery side dish—Crazy Bread. This warm garlic-infused bread was so good that I enjoyed it more than the pizza itself.

Yum!Yum!

Little Caesars also has a catchy phrase and memorable mascot. I remember Caesar slamming his pole down informing me of the latest Pizza!Pizza! or Pan!Pan! (now DEEP!DEEP!). A catchphrase and mascot will only take you so far, though; you need to deliver on the pizza. Thankfully, Little Caesars has always managed to pull that off.

ESTABLISHED	1969	SPECIALTY ITEMS		SECRET MENU ITEMS
FOUNDER	Jim Patterson	2 Fish Meal		Fried Crumbs (they're
GAME CHANGER	Hushpuppies	Hushpuppies		free)
FIRST LOCATION	Lexington, Kentucky	Popcorn Shrimp		
TOTAL LOCATIONS	Over 1,100			
TRADEMARK	Captain's Bell			
MASCOT	Long John Silver	SEASONAL SPECIALS		
CURRENT SLOGAN	America's Fish Fry	Lobster Bites		BEST
		Thick Cut Cod Basket		Fish (3)
CLASSIC SLOGAN	Go Fish	MUST HAVE		
		Hushpuppies		

One Fish, Two Fish

J im Patterson returned from an overseas vacation in 1969 where he had an exceptional fish and chips meal. He became a man on a mission—to bring his experience to America so we could share in fried fish goodness. Thus began the saga of Long John Silver's and its speedy expansion across the United States. It was hard to miss a Long John Silver's Seafood Shoppe. Each restaurant had a steeple on its roof and looked like a Cape Cod cottage. If you enjoyed your meal, there was a captain's bell to ring when you left the restaurant. Pirate hats and other treasures made Long John Silver's all about fun.

Fish and chips diversified into offerings of other seafood, chicken, and sides like corn on the cob or onion rings. The reason to go to Long John Silver's was its battered fried flaky fish, but it had a unique side item that eventually stood out on its own—hushpuppies. Whether combining fish, shrimp, chicken, or fries, hushpuppies were an absolute must for any Long John Silver's meal.

Long John Silver's was acquired by Yum! Brands, and combo restaurants with KFC began to spread across the land. Although ownership has since changed hands, the goal remains to keep the country thinking fish, and have people ringing the Captain's Bell after every meal.

Ring My Bell

As a Pittsburgh Pirates fan, a trip to Long John Silver's had added significance for me growing

Aargh . . . fish and chips, mateys!

Warning—kids will ring this bell regardless of fish performance.

up. In landlocked Pittsburgh, it felt like we were heading for the seas whenever we journeyed to this fish restaurant. I loved the fish and chips, but it was the free paper pirate hat that I was after. I wore that hat every time I exited, ringing the Captain's Bell whether or not I enjoyed the service.

Long John Silver's has transformed from a stand-alone chain of restaurants into a place you could only find grouped with other dining options. I miss those stand-alone cottages and hope to see them across the country once again.

McDonald's®

		SPECIALTY ITEMS	SECRET MENU ITEMS
ESTABLISHED	1948	Big Mac	Mc10:35
FOUNDERS	Dick & Mac McDonald	Quarter Pounder	All American
GAME CHANGER	Ray Kroc	Chicken McNuggets	Chicken & Waffles
FIRST LOCATION	San Bernardino, California	Filet-O-Fish	Land, Sea, and Air
		Egg McMuffin	McLeprechaun
		McFlurry	McKinley Mac
			Neapolitan
			Pie McFlurry

TOTAL LOCATIONS	Over 36,000		**BEST**
TRADEMARK	Golden Arches		Burgers (5)—*Double Quarter Pounder,*
MASCOT	Ronald McDonald	**SEASONAL SPECIALS**	Fries (2), Fish (4)—
CURRENT SLOGAN	I'm Lovin' It	McRib	*Filet-O-Fish,* Coffee (4),
		Shamrock Shake	Ice (4), Straws (1),
CLASSIC SLOGAN	You Deserve a Break Today		Drive-Thrus (4), Logos (1),
		MUST HAVE	Mascots (1)—*Ronald,*
		Large French Fries	Sweepstakes (1), Toy Collectibles (1)
			Slogans (2)—*You Deserve a Break Today,*
			Ad Campaigns (3),
			Secret Menus (3)
			OVERALL (1)

The Golden Arches

When Dick and Mac McDonald opened their Bar-B-Q restaurant in San Bernardino, California, in 1940, the brothers had no idea that they had begun to change the world. Eight years later, McDonald's reopened as a self-service drive-in using the "Speedee Service System" with nine items on its menu, which featured the 15-cent hamburger. The next year, French fries replaced potato chips and milkshakes made their debut. The core of the Golden Arches was in place.

Ray Kroc's first McDonald's, in Des Plaines, Illinois.

Milkshake mixer salesman Ray Kroc made his now legendary visit to the brothers in 1954 and agreed to franchise the historic hamburger joint, and the next year the Arches sprung up in Des Plaines, Illinois. By the end of the decade, McDonald's had sold its 275 millionth hamburger and operated 100 locations all over the country.

Ronald McDonald came on the scene in a mid-1960s national TV ad during the Macy's Thanksgiving Day Parade as the empire continued to grow. In 1968 the Big

Mac and Hot Apple Pie (both created by franchisees) were added to the national menu. Ronald was soon joined by Hamburglar, Grimace, Mayor McCheese, Captain Crook, and Officer Big Mac in McDonaldland, and McDonald's customers all "deserved a break today."

Saint Patrick's Day in 1970 is fondly remembered as the birthday of the Shamrock Shake. The Quarter Pounder (and Quarter Pounder with Cheese) made their respective debuts in 1973, and two years later the Egg McMuffin (another franchisee creation) brought breakfast to the Golden Arches.

Fry guys on the hunt for Mayor McCheese.

To make kids even more excited about a trip to Mickey D's, the Happy Meal made its debut in 1979. Chicken McNuggets came on the scene in 1983 as the menu continued to evolve. In the mid-1990s McDonald's supersized its menu, which led to some backlash and a Morgan Spurlock documentary. To the delight of apple farmers everywhere, fresh-cut apple slices are now included in every Happy Meal. Breakfast is available at all hours of the day. Thanks to these innovations, McDonald's has always managed to stay on top.

Billions Served

When I grew up in Mt. Lebanon, Pennsylvania, McDonald's was a half-mile walk away through my backyard. I took that stroll many times and grew to love the place. I remember my first Quarter Pounder like it was yesterday.

My beacon—the Golden Arches.

The Golden Arches made me a good student and definitely affected my behavior. I can remember getting an A on my report card and knowing that it meant a trip to McD's. After being a good boy at the dentist, my mom took me on a trip to see Ronald.

Unfortunately the fluoride hadn't worn off and Ronald ended up seeing me return his product on the floor, but that didn't stop me from going.

I avidly followed how many millions of burgers were served until McDonald's stopped counting and just called it at billions. I waited for the rare appearance of the Shamrock Shake—these days it's the McRib. My brother and I avidly searched for Monopoly game pieces, hoping to discover that elusive big-money property (we're still looking decades later). When driving around the country, if the Arches were in sight you knew exactly what meal you were in for.

I often felt that I deserved a break today. Ask anyone what's in a Big Mac, and without blinking they'll recite the ingredients as easy as "The Preamble" from

Two all-beef patties special sauce lettuce cheese pickles onions on a sesame seed bun.

Schoolhouse Rock! I still smile when I pull up to a McDonald's anticipating my Double Quarter Pounder without Cheese and those delicious fries. Consistency is the main reason for their success.

McDonald's is comforting, fun, and when those fries are "piping," it simply cannot be beat.

ESTABLISHED	1916	SPECIALTY ITEMS		SECRET MENU ITEMS
FOUNDER	Nathan Handwerker	World Famous Beef		
GAME CHANGER	Hot Dog	Hot Dog		
FIRST LOCATION	Coney Island, New York	Crinkle-Cut French Fries		
TOTAL LOCATIONS	Over 40,000			
TRADEMARK	Red Fry Fork			
MASCOT	HotDog	SEASONAL SPECIALS		
CURRENT SLOGAN	This Is The Original	Prime Rib		BEST
		Grille House Burger		Fries (1)
CLASSIC SLOGAN	The World's Best	MUST HAVE		Hot Dogs (1)
	Frankfurter	Hot Dog		
		French Fries		

World Famous Since 1916

Polish immigrant Nathan Handwerker opened a small frankfurter stand in Coney Island, New York, in 1916, selling hot dogs made with a recipe developed by his wife, Ida, for a nickel. A hundred years later, those one-of-a-kind Coney Island hot dogs are still pleasing millions of Americans.

Originally, Nathan's servers wore white surgeon's smocks to show cleanliness, and flyers were distributed to local hospitals inviting staff to eat for free. Nathan's

At Coney Island, I could eat all of this. I really could.

was an instant hit, with regular customers ranging from Al Capone to Cary Grant. FDR served Nathan's hot dogs to the king and queen of England in 1939. It's safe to say that Nathan's earned its title of "world famous."

Nathan's success was based on two simple principles—great-tasting hot dogs and inexpensive pricing. In 1946 Nathan's grew significantly in size and began to sell seafood products at its clam bar. In the 1950s, Nathan's son Murray began to expand the brand, opening stores in the metropolitan New York area. A taste of Coney Island was beginning to make its way through the country. Hot dogs are referred to as Coneys in many parts of the country, and Nathan's is the reason why.

These days when the Fourth of July rolls around, all eyes turn to Coney Island for the annual Hot Dog Eating Contest. As contestants wolf down a plethora of dogs, this Brooklyn landmark celebrates another year of success. I'm not sure what's in that water down at Coney Island, but if that's the secret ingredient that makes those hot dogs so scrumptious, I'm on board.

Boardwalk Empire

I remember my father taking our family to Nathan's in Coney Island every summer. Two plain hot dogs and an order of fries is all that

My daughter Rachel and me celebrating the Fourth at Coney Island.

I needed. It was such a special Hein family trip that I still make it with my dad and brother to celebrate Father's Day every year.

You can't help but feel nostalgic whenever you visit Nathan's. There are new menu offerings, but really nothing has changed all that much since 1916. The hot dog is what made Nathan's world famous, and the crinkle-cut fries (and that red fry fork) are also the best in the land. The size, texture, and taste of these fries are simply incredible.

I realize that everyone doesn't eat like I do, but when you go to Nathan's, you really should order a hot dog and fries . . . anything else would be sacrilegious.

The best fries you will ever taste.

		SPECIALTY ITEMS	SECRET MENU ITEMS
ESTABLISHED	1981	Sourdough Bread Bowl	Power Breakfast Salads
FOUNDERS	Louis Kane, Ken Rosenthal,	Broccoli Cheddar Soup	Power Chicken Hummus
	Ron Shaich	Fuji Apple Chicken Salad	Bowl
GAME CHANGER	You Pick Two	Mac & Cheese	
FIRST LOCATION	Kirkwood, Missouri	Cinnamon Crunch Bagel	
TOTAL LOCATIONS	Over 1,900	Bacon Turkey Bravo	
TRADEMARK	Fresh Bread	sandwich	
MASCOT		**SEASONAL SPECIALS**	
CURRENT SLOGAN	Make Today Better	Pink Ribbon Bagel	**BEST**
		Strawberry Poppyseed &	
		Chicken Salad	
CLASSIC SLOGAN	A Loaf of Bread in	**MUST HAVE**	
	Every Arm	Grilled Cheese	

Filling Up on Bread

My parents always warned me to never fill up on bread. At Panera Bread, it's okay to make an exception. The roots of Panera Bread can be traced back to Au Bon Pain Co., which began in 1981. Au Bon Pain acquired the Saint Louis Bread Company, a chain of 20 bakery-cafès in the greater St. Louis area. This brand was so successful that Au Bon Pain Co. sold all of its other units and renamed its company Panera

Wish this was scratch and sniff.

Bread. They've been baking fresh bread and prospering ever since. (Another company has since bought and used the name Au Bon Pain.)

Panera Bread defies the fast food stereotype, priding itself on serving wholesome meals that taste delicious. All Panera locations have a fresh, healthy menu. Panera Bread was the first national restaurant chain to voluntarily disclose caloric content on menu panels.

And Panera isn't just bread. It offers a variety of sandwiches, salads, panini, and pasta dishes. Its allure is the fresh-baked bread, but what you put on it is just as important. Its most unique offering is a bread bowl, an ingenious use of bread where they pour your favorite soup right inside. After you finish your warm soup, you get to devour the bowl itself. Brilliantly efficient.

Baked Fresh Every Morning

I admit it, before I ever set foot inside a Panera Bread, I thought it was simply a bread store. I took the brand name literally. Don't get me wrong, nothing beats the smell of a freshly baked loaf of bread (and Panera knows it), though the store offers a variety of food items to its customers.

But if it's bread variety that you're looking for, Panera has it. Whole Grain, Three Cheese, Ciabatta, Cinnamon Raisin Swirl, or All-Natural White—all baked fresh

Very tasty grilled cheese.

Bread Bowl—it's all edible.

daily at Panera and donated to local food pantries if unsold at the end of the day. When it comes to grilled cheese, it's nice to have different breads to choose from.

The You Pick Two combo gets you the best of both worlds. You can choose two of the following—half pasta, cup of soup, half sandwich, or half salad—and create your own meal. Ultimately, Panera makes you feel healthy when you sample its fresh offerings, and that's what this bakery-café is all about.

Better Ingredients.
Better Pizza.

ESTABLISHED	1983
FOUNDER	John Schnatter
GAME CHANGER	Online Ordering
FIRST LOCATION	Jeffersonville, Indiana
TOTAL LOCATIONS	Over 4,600
TRADEMARK	The Camaro Z28
MASCOT	Papa John
CURRENT SLOGAN	Better Ingredients. Better Pizza.
CLASSIC SLOGAN	Better Ingredients. Better Pizza.

SPECIALTY ITEMS
The Works
Spicy Italian
Sausage
Garlic Parmesan
Breadsticks

SEASONAL SPECIALS
Buffalo Chicken
Double Cheeseburger

MUST HAVE
The Works

SECRET MENU ITEMS
Cinnapie

BEST
Pizza (4)
Sweepstakes (4)

Bitchin' Camaro

Young John Schnatter treasured two things—making pizza and his 1971 Camaro Z28. In 1983 John knocked out a broom closet in the back of his father's tavern, Mick's Lounge in Jeffersonville, Indiana. He sold his prized Camaro to buy used pizza-making equipment and began selling pies out of his converted closet. Papa John's had arrived, and in only one year the pizza proved to be so popular that John was moving to his first restaurant in an adjoining space.

When he delivered pizza on campus as a student, John felt the national pizza chains were missing something—a superior-quality pizza with better ingredients that could be delivered to homes. Fresh dough and those high-end ingredients would be critical to Papa John's success, and the franchise has quickly grown into the third-largest takeout and pizza delivery chain in the United States.

Technology is what put Papa John's over the top. It was the first pizza chain to make online ordering available to all of its customers. Getting there first was critical, but meaningless without the product to back it up. Papa John's pizza menu is always evolving, trying different combinations, like bacon and BBQ sauce or pulled pork and pineapple, to please its customers without sacrificing any quality.

Better Ingredients. Better Pizza.

You can't miss the man behind the pizza, John Schnatter. He is everywhere. Some may find the pizza maven annoying. Some may find him appealing. But you can't miss him. Papa John's has made the most out of its marketing. There is not a channel or sporting event that doesn't involve Papa John's in some way. Bowl games, stadiums, Final Fours . . . you will find Papa John's there.

It is difficult to crack the pizza market, and Papa John's did it by differentiating itself. John Schnatter grew up on pizza, studied pizza, and learned what it takes with his own two hands. His energy, and pizza, are infectious.

The thing I like best about

Come to Papa!

Papa John's is how easy it is to customize your pizza. There's also the standard menu to order from, but no topping combination is too crazy for this place. Many of its standard menu items were created by popular combinations from customers. Whenever a restaurant puts the order in my hands, I get excited. Thanks, Papa.

Pizza Hut

ESTABLISHED	1958	SPECIALTY ITEMS		SECRET MENU ITEMS
FOUNDERS	Dan & Frank Carney	Hand Tossed		
GAME CHANGER	The Hut	Stuffed Crust		
FIRST LOCATION	Wichita, Kansas	Ultimate Cheese Lover's		
TOTAL LOCATIONS	Over 15,000	P'Zone		
TRADEMARK	Red Roof	Cheese Sticks		
MASCOT	Pete	SEASONAL SPECIALS		
CURRENT SLOGAN	Flavor of Now	Double Deep		BEST
		Garlic Parmesan		Pizza (2)
CLASSIC SLOGAN	Now You're Eating!	MUST HAVE		
		Stuffed Crust Pizza		
		Buffet		

Wichita Linemen

In 1958 a friend of Dan and Frank Carney suggested opening a pizza parlor—a rarity those days in Wichita, Kansas. The brothers thought this was a feasible idea, so they borrowed $600 from their mother and set up shop in a brick building on the Wichita State University campus. They called their new restaurant Pizza Hut. On opening night they gave away free pizza to generate interest, and within a year they had opened their first franchise, in Topeka, then quickly expanded across the nation.

Distinctive red roofs began to pop up everywhere serving warm pizza at comfortable dine-in locations. You didn't have to be in New York or Chicago to grab a slice.

Over the years, salads, breadsticks, and pastas were added to the menu. Pizza Hut also experimented with different types of pizza, changing crusts, toppings, and sizes to keep things interesting. The Hut instituted the Personal Pan Pizza and was behind the stuffed crust movement, ranging from cheese to hot dogs embedded inside the outside of your pizza.

The logo you couldn't miss across the country.

In the 1980s Pizza Hut moved into the delivery/carryout space and a fast food express model. You didn't have to sit down in a Pizza Hut to get your pizza anymore. After being acquired by Yum! Brands, which owns KFC and other fast food chains, Pizza Hut began to offer WingStreet Wings along with its other items.

Get Stuffed

Stuffed crust pizza—a game changer for the Hut.

Fast food restaurants are constantly evolving, but it's rare to see a true game changer in the pizza world. I mean, how many different toppings can you really come up with? So instead of altering the pie toppings, the Hut decided to reinvent the pizza crust by stuffing it. I'll never turn down more cheese in my cheese pizza! But Pizza Hut didn't stop there. Their pizzas are now stuffed with not just one cheese, but three. Or with pretzels. Or hot dogs. Bacon has got to be up next. Fill 'er up!

POPEYES
✦ LOUISIANA KITCHEN ✦

		SPECIALTY ITEMS	SECRET MENU ITEMS
ESTABLISHED	1972	Bonafide Spicy Chicken	Deep Fried Apple Pie
FOUNDER	Al Copeland	Buttermilk Biscuits	Naked Chicken
GAME CHANGER	Cajun Style	Chicken Po'Boy	
FIRST LOCATION	Arabi, Louisiana	Cajun Fries	
TOTAL LOCATIONS	Over 2,400	Jambalaya	
TRADEMARK	Spicy Chicken		
MASCOT	Annie the Chicken Queen	**SEASONAL SPECIALS**	**BEST**
CURRENT SLOGAN	Love That Chicken	Seafood Mardi Gras	Fried Chicken (3)
		Wicked Chicken	Biscuits (2)
CLASSIC SLOGAN	Louisiana Fast	**MUST HAVE**	
		Bonafide Spicy Chicken	
		Buttermilk Biscuits	

French Connection

In 1972 Al Copeland opened Chicken on the Run in the New Orleans suburb of Arabi, where he served traditional southern-fried chicken. A few months passed and nothing much happened, so he decided to sell spicy New Orleans–style chicken and call the place Popeyes. The name wasn't based on the spinach-eating cartoon sailor, but rather on Gene Hackman's memorable detective Popeye Doyle from the classic film

Popeyes' nectar.

The French Connection. Copeland claimed he was too poor to afford an apostrophe for Popeyes and luckily had no trademark issues to deal with.

Sales took off as this Cajun-style chicken offered a spicy alternative to the original recipe of Colonel Sanders. Popeyes quickly expanded in the 1980s, adding buttermilk biscuits and crawfish to its menu. The tastes of New Orleans were traveling all over the United States. Popeyes and Church's were both acquired by larger entities to expand this spicy chicken idea, and growth hasn't slowed for the Louisiana Kitchen.

Jambalaya, red beans and rice, and other spicy flavors have been added to the menu along with po'boys and other Cajun offerings, but ultimately customers keep coming back for that spicy New Orleans–style chicken.

Louisiana Purchase

Al Copeland learned firsthand that you can't beat the Colonel at his own game. Standard chicken recipes won't cut it, but spicy chicken can make a mark. Kentucky Fried Chicken added its Extra Crispy option in response to Popeyes' success. And Popeyes has never shied away from its Louisiana branding.

Cajun chicken, biscuit, and fries—classic Popeyes.

Unlike Kentucky, Louisiana is known for its spicy meals, and Popeyes chicken reflects this in its herbs and spices, which have much more of a kick than the Colonel's original recipe. A drink is an absolute must-have at Popeyes to wash your bird down.

I'm partial to the Colonel's Original Recipe, but when I'm looking to spice up the poultry, Popeyes offers my bird of choice. The Cajun crispiness and buttermilk biscuits make a fine fast food fried chicken meal.

ESTABLISHED	1995	SPECIALTY ITEMS		SECRET MENU ITEMS
FOUNDERS	Anthony Miller & Robert Hauser	Burrito Craft 2 Grilled Quesadilla 3-Cheese Queso		
GAME CHANGER	Mission-Style Burritos			
FIRST LOCATION	Denver, Colorado			
TOTAL LOCATIONS	Over 600			
TRADEMARK	San Francisco Burrito Style			
MASCOT		SEASONAL SPECIALS		
CURRENT SLOGAN	We Live Food	Queso for a Kiss Mango Chicken Salad		BEST Tacos (2) Burritos (5)
CLASSIC SLOGAN	Not Just Big Burritos. Big Flavors.	MUST HAVE Chicken Queso Burrito Guacamole		

What's in a Name?

It took a few tries to get the name right, but Qdoba (kew-DOH-buh) Mexican Grill has become a formidable competitor in the growing space of Mexican fast food. Anthony Miller and Robert Hauser opened their restaurant, Zuma, in Denver, Colorado, in 1995. (Chipotle also got its start in Denver, so maybe there's just something in that mile-high air.) Other Zuma Mexican restaurants forced a name change to Z-Teca,

Your friendly neighborhood Qdoba.

but that was too similar to existing Z'Tejas restaurants. An ad agency created the name Qdoba to ensure that there was no more brand confusion. This was a made-up word that sounded foreign and began with a *Q*—perfect.

Regardless of what you called the place, this Mexican Grill was an immediate success and soon expanding. Qdoba has always served its food San Francisco burrito style (large size with extra rice and other ingredients), which distinguishes itself in the market. There are no secret menu items, because you're building your own meal each time you go to Qdoba—the entire menu is a secret menu for the taking! The guacamole and queso are especially fresh.

Jack in the Box acquired Qdoba in 2003 and has expanded the brand even further nationwide. Qdoba now also serves breakfast burritos to help distinguish itself from its Mexican-style competition.

Mexican Standoff

Qdoba versus Chipotle. Both restaurants originated in Colorado and offer fresh Mexican-style food. So other than the name, what's the difference between the two growing giants?

Both restaurants are very good at what they do. The food is made fresh right in front of your

Customize a Qdoba burrito any way you'd like.

Qdoba Queso and Guac

eyes with inviting kitchens. Qdoba provides a few more options for customization than the spicier Chipotle does. But you can't go wrong with either place.

If you love your queso, then Qdoba is your choice. They offer different types of warm queso, like 3-Cheese or Diablo, to spice up your meal. Plus, the *Q* alliteration makes ordering queso at Qdoba all the more fun.

ESTABLISHED	1981	SPECIALTY ITEMS	SECRET MENU ITEMS
FOUNDERS	Terrell Braly, Jimmy Lambatos, Todd Disner	Classic Italian	
		Honey Bourbon Chicken	
GAME CHANGER	Toasted Subs	Mesquite Chicken	
		Chicken Carbonara	
FIRST LOCATION	Denver, Colorado	Turkey Ranch & Swiss	
TOTAL LOCATIONS	Over 2,000		
TRADEMARK	Toasted Subs		
MASCOT	Spongmonkeys (old school)	SEASONAL SPECIALS	
CURRENT SLOGAN	Mmmm . . . Toasty!	Lobster & Seafood Salad Sub	BEST
		Chicken Fajita Sub	
CLASSIC SLOGAN	Made Easy	MUST HAVE	
		Classic Italian	

Toasty Difference

What can you make of an abandoned Sinclair gas station in Denver, Colorado? The second-largest sub sandwich company in the country. In 1978 Terrell Braly turned the lot into Sandwich World and toasted sandwiches in an old pizza oven. Braly sold to competitors Jimmy Lambatos and Todd Disner, who turned the place into Quiznos Subs in 1981. The made-up name sounded Italian, but the sandwiches were created by culinary-trained chefs. Hot subs on toasted breads is the magic formula for Quiznos. Ten years later, Rick Schaden and his father bought the franchise and began to expand the toasty brand.

Quiznos positioned itself as the place for high-end sub sandwiches where quality came first. You paid more, but you got a better sandwich. Ingredients were always fresh, but it was the toasted bread that made the difference at Quiznos. The subs were inspired by oven-baked sandwiches from New York. These toasted subs provided a true competitor to the mighty Subway, and Quiznos grew at a very rapid rate.

Oven-baked classics contin-ued to please customers, and soon the "Subs" was dropped from the company name and Quiznos stood alone. A Super Bowl ad in the early 2000s with the bizarre Spongmon-keys further launched the brand, and Quiznos was growing at the rate of one store per day. Soups and salads have always been designed

The first Quiznos—a converted Sinclair gas station.

to complement its signature subs, and Quiznos now offers flatbreads as well. But customers keep coming back for that warm bread, something Quiznos will never change.

Quiznos got away from making "high-end" sandwiches, a mistake that led the chain to declare bankruptcy. Quiznos can come back, though—they just need to re-turn to that toaster oven and let the sandwiches do the talking. It is very difficult to make a bad sandwich on warm, toasted bread.

Come to Quiznos!

Subway dominates the fast food world of subs, but being number two isn't too bad. Just ask Burger King how it feels about McDonald's. There's plenty of room

The Classic Italian—Quiznos' best sub.

for everyone. For a short time, it seemed that Quiznos could compete with Subway thanks to its toasting, but Subway's pricing keeps them on top.

Another thing that sets Quiznos apart is its unique advertising. The Spongmonkeys were arguably the most bizarre fast food mascots ever created (the King from BK is still the scariest). No one knew what they were in 2004, but Quiznos got noticed. The goal was to get us into the sub shop and let the toaster do the rest—smart advertising.

Roy Rogers®

ESTABLISHED	1968	**SPECIALTY ITEMS**		**SECRET MENU ITEMS**	
FOUNDER	Peter Plamondon	Roast Beef Sandwich			
GAME CHANGER	Fixin's Bar	Fried Chicken			
FIRST LOCATION	Falls Church, Virginia	Double R Bar Burger			
TOTAL LOCATIONS	Over 50				
TRADEMARK	Roy				
MASCOT	Roy Rogers	**SEASONAL SPECIALS**			
CURRENT SLOGAN	Roy Rogers Rides Again	Pumpkin Shake		**BEST**	
CLASSIC SLOGAN	Fast Food Done Right	**MUST HAVE**		Fried Chicken (2)	
		Fried Chicken			

Happy Trails

Peter Plamondon was an executive with the Marriott Corporation who wanted to open a fast food restaurant that offered people a choice of the big three—hamburgers, roast beef sandwiches, or fried chicken. Marriott converted the Hot Shoppes Jr. fast food chain to a new all-American name that they licensed—Roy Rogers. The first location opened in Falls Church, Virginia, in 1968 with Roy's promise as its cornerstone: "There's no reason in the world why you can't get good food even if you're in a hurry."

The chain flourished for Marriott, which began to open Roy's all throughout the Northeast in the 1970s. Roy Rogers excelled at each of its big three items. The Double R Bar burger was a solid offering, the roast beef sandwich was on a par with Arby's, and the fried chicken was comparable to the Colonel's. Roy's also offered a Fixin's Bar, which contained unlimited vegetables and sauces to add to your sandwich. It was a recipe for success.

Roy's was ahead of its time with its Fixin's Bar.

In 1990 Marriott sold its successful chain to Hardee's, which used the Roy Rogers fried chicken recipe to compete with Kentucky Fried Chicken. Most locations were being coverted to Hardee's, but Roy Rogers customers revolted and eventually these sites returned to being Roy's locations. Flame-broiled hamburgers were offered, but Roy's customers wanted things the way they used to be. Hardee's eventually sold off the locations to other competitors, leaving a handful of Roy Rogers restaurants (many of which are located at New Jersey Turnpike rest stops; I guess they made a long-term deal).

Peter Plamondon's sons reacquired the franchise rights and relaunched Roy Rogers with lines out the door. The company is currently on the rebound and back to offering the big three.

Roy Rogers Rides Again

Roy Rogers holds a special place in my heart. I remember my seventh birthday party being held at a Roy Rogers in Green Tree, Pennsylvania. My name up on that big sign is forever etched into my memory. But I also love Roy's because of its fried chicken. This special recipe created a crispy alternative to Kentucky Fried Chicken that tasted just as good. Its roast beef sandwich was on a par with Arby's, and the burgers . . . well, two out of three ain't bad.

Roy Rogers has a devout cult-like following (like Apple, without the tech), and as the brand is relaunched, customers will come back if the food lives up to its billing. I hope the Plamondons stay true to what made Roy's so special and restore this fast food franchise to its rightful place.

It's a tough act to follow, but Roy Rogers could ride again. My many stops at New Jersey Turnpike rest areas on the way home from Atlantic City can attest to that.

Roy's has some of the best fried chicken you'll ever taste.

ESTABLISHED	1956	SPECIALTY ITEMS		SECRET MENU ITEMS
FOUNDERS	Gennaro & Carmela Sbarro	New York Pizza		
GAME CHANGER	New York Style Pizza	Stromboli		
FIRST LOCATION	Brooklyn, New York	Sicilian Pizza		
TOTAL LOCATIONS	Over 800	Garlic Breadsticks		
TRADEMARK	The Flag			
MASCOT				
CURRENT SLOGAN	New York Style	SEASONAL SPECIALS		BEST
		Spicy Italian Pizza		
		Chicken Bacon Ranch Pizza		
CLASSIC SLOGAN	We Don't Cut Corners	MUST HAVE		
		4 Cheese		

Straight Out of Brooklyn

In 1956, Italian immigrants Gennaro and Carmela Sbarro opened their first salumeria (Italian grocery store) in Brooklyn, New York, which became popular for its fresh food. The Italian grocery opened more locations in the metropolitan New York area with great success. In 1970, Sbarro opened its first restaurant in a mall, a decision that would shape the company forever.

The concept was simple: an open kitchen making Italian food that was available for fast service. As Sbarro grew into much more than a Brooklyn salumeria, department stores, airports, malls, and similar locations with food courts soon had a Sbarro to offer Italian fare.

If there's a mall, there's a Sbarro.

Many people think Sbarro is simply a pizza place, but it has always been an Italian eatery. Spaghetti, lasagna, or baked ziti are all served with Carmela Sbarro's signature sauce. New York–style pizza slices are Sbarro's most popular offering, though, primarily because they are the quickest item to purchase.

Sbarro has been in and out of bankruptcy with the fast-casual market starting to catch up to its model. But its reach remains tremendous, and chances are that if you're in a mall, you'll find Sbarro.

New York Style

As a New Yorker, I'm very defensive when it comes to pizza. Don't get me wrong, I love Chicago deep dish and other styles, but there's nothing better than a fresh slice of New York pizza. Sbarro does not offer New York pizza—it offers New York–"style" pizza.

I can't tell you if it's the water, the sauce, or the dough, but New York pizza is next to impossible to re-create outside of New York. Sbarro offers a version of New York pizza that works if you're nowhere near the five boroughs.

A great quick snack at the mall.

When you're at the mall, you look for something that you can get on the go. That is what Sbarro does best. It's no salumeria, but it's hot, it's fresh, and it's Italian. That's Sbarro.

ESTABLISHED	1953	SPECIALTY ITEMS	SECRET MENU ITEMS
FOUNDER	Troy Smith	SuperSONIC Bacon Double Cheeseburger	Dr Pepper Orgasm
GAME CHANGER	Drive-In	Chili Cheese Coney Dog	Frito Pie
FIRST LOCATION	Shawnee, Oklahoma	Tots	Grilled Ham & Cheese
TOTAL LOCATIONS	Over 3,500	Limeade	
TRADEMARK	Carhops		
MASCOT		**SEASONAL SPECIALS**	**BEST**
CURRENT SLOGAN	This Is How You Sonic	SuperSONIC Breakfast Burrito	Beverages (2)—*Cherry Limeade*
		Banana Shake	Hot Dogs (5)
CLASSIC SLOGAN	Service at the Speed of Sound	**MUST HAVE**	Chili (4)
		Tots	Ice (1)
		Cherry Limeade	Uniforms (1)
		Ice	

America's Drive-In

Troy Smith opened a hamburger and root beer stand in 1953 in Shawnee, Oklahoma, called Top Hat Drive-In. The restaurant's unique feature was curbside speakers that allowed customers to place their orders without ever leaving their car. This technology, service at the speed of sound, translated into one word that made

The sign for America's Drive-In.

a lot of sense—*Sonic.* So Troy Smith changed his restaurant's name in 1959, and Sonic has continued to deliver food to our cars with the help of some roller skates.

Personal carhop service has always been a Sonic staple and one of the many reasons customers keep pulling in. It's the only national drive-in that thrives in today's world of fast food. Roller-skating waiters or waitresses capture the fun that is Sonic, and they're always smiling and making sure your order is safe and correct. Each customer receives a mint with any drink, dessert, or meal purchase, a tradition started by Troy Smith to remind customers that they're worth a mint at Sonic.

Sonic's menu has broadened over the years as the brand expands and continues to amass locations. Sonic sells enough Tots that, when placed end to end, they would circle the globe . . . twice. The onion rings at Sonic are sliced, breaded, and cooked fresh every day on the premises. Everything is customizable at Sonic, and its menu is available 24/7 to any car that pulls up with hungry customers. That is how you Sonic.

This Is How I Sonic-ed

I got to try my luck as a Carhop at Sonic down in its home state of Oklahoma, and it is a lot more difficult than it looks. You might think you're a good skater, but when you're skating with Limeades and Tots, it's

It's me, your friendly Sonic Carhop.

a whole different story. My skating was rusty, but I managed to stay upright for most of my training.

Sonic is all about a good time. There has always been something cool about ordering through a speaker and having your meal brought to you by a carhop on skates. You simply can't get that drive-in experience anywhere else these days. And there are so many combinations of food and drink to create at Sonic, it's never the same meal twice.

Ice, ice, baby.

Sonic bills itself as the Ultimate Drink Stop, and it's earned that right with over 1 million drink and slush combinations available. If it's summertime, the summer of shakes leaves you with options like Oreo or Cookie Dough and 50 total slush or shake flavors.

But the most amazing thing about Sonic is its ice. Customers will come in and order the ice for their coolers, paying around two bucks for a ten-pound bag, because it lasts longer than any other ice you can find. I don't know what's in those pellets, but it is a marvel of engineering that has made many tailgaters quite happy.

TM

ESTABLISHED	1971
FOUNDERS	Jerry Baldwin, Zev Siegl, Gordon Bowker
GAME CHANGER	Fresh Roasted Whole Bean Coffee
FIRST LOCATION	Seattle, Washington
TOTAL LOCATIONS	Over 22,500

TRADEMARK	The Siren's Eye
MASCOT	The Siren
CURRENT SLOGAN	
CLASSIC SLOGAN	Life Happens Over Coffee

SPECIALTY ITEMS
Brewed Coffee
Sumatra
Pike Place
Vanilla Latte
Caramel Macchiato
Double Chocolaty Chip
   Frappuccino
Iced Coffee

SEASONAL SPECIALS
Pumpkin Spice Latte
Holiday Blend

MUST HAVE
Vanilla Latte
Passion Tea Lemonade

SECRET MENU ITEMS
Black Eye
Cake Batter Frappuccino
Chocolate Dalmatian
Dirty Chai
Green Eye
Raspberry Cheesecake
Red Eye
Short Drink
Thin Mint Frappuccino
Triple C's
Zebra Mocha

BEST
Coffee (1)
Beverages (3)—*Passion
   Tea Lemonade*
Pastries (5)
Straws (3)
Logos (3)
Secret Menus (2)
Uniforms (5)

Call Me Ishmael

The first Starbucks was opened at Pike Place Market in Seattle, Washington, in 1971 by three guys who had met at the University of San Francisco. The trio was inspired to sell high-quality coffee beans, and after rejecting the name *Pequod* (the whaling ship from *Moby-Dick*), they settled on that ship's first mate's name, Starbuck.

The company sold roasted whole coffee beans, but only brewed coffee in the store as free samples. As total sales of coffee fell but specialty coffee sales increased, former employee Howard Schultz purchased Starbucks from the original owners in 1987 and began selling the coffee and expanding. Since this acquisition, Starbucks has opened, on average, two new stores every day. That's a lot of java.

Specialty coffees became the rage for the next decade, and Starbucks rode this wave to immense popularity. Its whole bean coffee was just better than most other storefront brands, but Starbucks

A good sign at the original Starbucks.

didn't stop there. The coffee giant now serves whole bean coffee, instant coffee, teas, different beverages, pastries, and snacks. Its coffeehouses manned by baristas have become a place to hang out with free Wi-Fi and a good vibe. Starbucks also offers plenty of seasonal drinks, so whether it's winter or summer, customer thirsts can always be quenched.

There are so many variations of drinks to get at Starbucks, it is impossible to keep up with at times. As a result, Starbucks has one of the most extensive unofficial secret menus in the world of fast food (check out my Secret Menu Items Dossier, pages 267–268, for a full list).

More Than a Cup of Joe

I'm no coffee drinker, but Starbucks blows me away. It's one thing to preach a Seattle earthy vibe, but Starbucks pulls it off at its many locations across the globe.

Starbucks has accomplished what all fast food places strive for—having customers willing to just hang in their space all day. Whether it's DQ or Wendy's, most renovated fast food locations are following Starbucks' successful model: hot coffee and free Wi-Fi. A customer who stays is one who will eventually pay.

With over 22,500 locations worldwide, Starbucks continues to grow at an insane rate and carry out its mission—to inspire and nurture the human spirit one person, one cup, and one neighborhood at a time.

A not-so-simple cup of coffee.

		SECRET MENU ITEMS
ESTABLISHED 1934	**SPECIALTY ITEMS**	
FOUNDER Gus Belt	The Original Double 'N Cheese	
GAME CHANGER Steakburgers	Classic Vanilla Milkshake	
FIRST LOCATION Normal, Illinois	4 Dollar Footlong	
TOTAL LOCATIONS Over 500	Thin 'N Crispy Fries	
TRADEMARK Steakburgers	5-Way Chili	
	Frisco Melt	
	7x7	
MASCOTS Sizzle, Goldie & Shaker	**SEASONAL SPECIALS**	
CURRENT SLOGAN Famous for Steakburgers	EggNog Milkshake	**BEST**
	Oktoberfest Steakburger	Milkshakes (4)—*Vanilla*
CLASSIC SLOGAN In Sight It Must Be Right	**MUST HAVE**	
	Any Milkshake	
	Chili Cheese Fries	

In Sight It Must Be Right

When Gus Belt converted a gas station/chicken restaurant in Normal, Illinois, into a hamburger stand in 1934, he came up with a straightforward name—Steak 'n Shake. Gus would wait for the busiest time and then grind steak right in front of any skeptical customers to prove how fresh his burgers were, generating the slogan "In Sight It Must Be Right." Gus would also put shake machines in the windows of his restaurant to tempt passersby into having a milkshake.

Fierce demand led to Gus expanding Steak 'n Shake to neighboring states, making sure that quality Steakburgers and shakes were available to all. He added curb service because every restaurant had a never-ending line to get inside and grab a seat. In the 1970s, drive-thrus replaced curb service as fast food competition heated up all over the country.

E. W. "Ed" Kelley took over in 1981 and returned Steak 'n Shake to its roots, including made-to-order meals served to guests on real china. Melts were added to the

The Original Double 'N Cheese

menu, but the biggest change was keeping the restaurants open 24 hours a day, 7 days a week. These changes got Steak 'n Shake growing again, and the throwback feeling of each location is as comforting to customers as those burgers and shakes always have been.

It's All in the Name

When I first encountered Steak 'n Shake in St. Louis, Missouri, the restaurant's name dictated my order. I enjoyed my Steakburger and fries, but I adored the shake. You can always taste the difference in a fresh, handspun milkshake, and Steak 'n Shake has a ton of different combinations to choose from. Start with the Classic Vanilla Milkshake and go from there.

A classic vanilla milkshake.

Steak 'n Shake has a throwback feel to it. Meals aren't delivered on china any-more, but it wouldn't surprise me if they brought that back. Burgers, melts, chili, and hot dogs give Steak 'n Shake the appeal of a diner in a fast food restaurant. Signature restaurants are smaller higher-end counter-service restaurants in markets without a Steak 'n Shake.

A great option at Steak 'n Shake is its unique Up All Night menu. Dishes like the Steakburger Slinger, Chili Cheese Fries, and the 7x7 (7 Steakburgers and 7 slices of cheese) are available for late-night munching (sharing is optional). No matter what time you show up at Steak 'n Shake, you can always count on getting a good burger, some warm fries, and a delicious shake.

ESTABLISHED	1965	SPECIALTY ITEMS		SECRET MENU ITEMS	
FOUNDERS	Fred DeLuca &	Italian B.M.T.		Old Cut	
	Dr. Peter Buck	Subway Club		Pizza Sub	
GAME CHANGER	The B.M.T.	Subway Melt			
FIRST LOCATION	Bridgeport, Connecticut	Meatball Marinara			
		Chicken & Bacon Ranch			
TOTAL LOCATIONS	Over 43,500				
TRADEMARK	$5 Footlong			**BEST**	
MASCOT		**SEASONAL SPECIALS**		Straws (2)	
CURRENT SLOGAN	Eat Fresh	Smokehouse BBQ		Sandwiches (5)—*Italian*	
		Chicken Sub		*B.M.T.*	
		FebruANY Footlongs		Ad Campaigns (5)	
				Slogans (3)—*Eat Fresh*	
CLASSIC SLOGAN	The Way a Sandwich	**MUST HAVE**		Sweepstakes (5)	
	Should Be	The B.M.T.			

Super Submarines

In 1965 seventeen-year-old Fred DeLuca and family friend Dr. Peter Buck teamed up to open their first submarine sandwich shop, called Pete's Super Submarines, in Bridgeport, Connecticut. Fred was hoping to earn enough money to pay his college tuition and eventually become a doctor. Three years later, the successful shop was renamed Subway with arrows on the ends of the *S* and *Y* in tribute to the New

The first store, in Bridgeport, Connecticut, opened in 1965. A name change
and many more locations would soon follow.

York City subway system. In 1974 the first Subway franchise opened in Wallingford, Connecticut, and began the climb to becoming the largest fast food operation in the world today. The next year, Subway's best-selling sub was introduced: the B.M.T., which originally was named for the Brooklyn–Manhattan Transit system (it's now referred to as Biggest, Meatiest, Tastiest).

Subway continued to open in a variety of locations across the country, and they also continued to innovate. In the 1970s, Subway introduced the Snak, which eventually became the six-inch sub. The early 1980s brought freshly baked bread, and Sand-wich Artists (as their employees are known) were constantly busy serving customers. Equipment re-quirements were, and continue to be, minimal, allowing Subway res-taurants to open in the tightest of spaces. But the quality of the subs has always remained consistent.

One of 43,500-plus locations around the world.

Toasted subs and $5 foot-longs have become staples of the

franchise's cuisine, and with over 43,500 locations, Subway sits atop the fast food restaurant rankings these days.

Sandwich Artists

My favorite part of eating at Subway is actually the ordering. There is an art to it, so it's no wonder they call the folks behind the counter "Sandwich Artists." When you first enter a Subway, take a close look at "the line." The line is the team assembled to make your sandwich quickly and efficiently. There's the leadoff spot, who takes your order, selects your bread, and makes the critical cut. Next is the "what kind of meat" person, who starts to assemble your sandwich.

Eat fresh!

The "middle of the order" puts on your toppings and completes your sandwich by tucking it into the bag. Last, but not least, there's the register, who takes your money and wishes you a good day.

A good lineup is critical to a successful trip at Subway. If you notice talent on the line, be sure to compliment it. Being a Sandwich Artist is no easy job. Also, keep your spot on the line. If you get bypassed for toasting, follow your sandwich. It's easy to get lost in the fray. Once you find a Subway with a solid lineup, treasure it.

Your food is always right in front of you at Subway. You can ask (and pay) for double meat if you feel your sub isn't enough. Don't hesitate to ask for extra veggies though—no charge for that—as long as the line keeps moving. Eat fresh!

TACO BELL®

ESTABLISHED	1962	SPECIALTY ITEMS	SECRET MENU ITEMS
FOUNDER	Glen Bell	Crunchy Taco Supreme	Cheesarito
GAME CHANGER	Bell Beefer	Cheesy Gordita Crunch	Double Grilled
FIRST LOCATION	Downey, California	Doritos Locos Taco	Quesadilla
TOTAL LOCATIONS	Over 6,200	Crunchwrap Supreme	Enchirito
		Nachos Supreme	The Hulk
			Quesarito
			Superman
TRADEMARK	Crunchy Beef Taco		BEST
MASCOT	Gidget the Chihuahua	SEASONAL SPECIALS	Tacos (1)
CURRENT SLOGAN	Live Más	Chili Cheese Burrito	Burritos (4)
		Beefy Crunch Burrito	Drive-Thrus (3)
			Ad Campaigns (1)
CLASSIC SLOGAN	Think Outside the Bun	MUST HAVE	Secret Menus (4)
		Crunchwrap Supreme	Toy Collectibles (5)

Ding Ding

Glen Bell started Bell's Burgers in California during the 1950s with the idea that customers could walk up and get their food from a service window. But as the West Coast burger market got more and more crowded, Bell sensed it was time for his next big idea: tacos. Few Americans were aware of what tacos were, but Glen

A blissful crunchy taco.

had tried them in Mexico and knew he could bring them to America using a hard, crunchy shell. He opened Taco Tia, which was an instant hit, and later El Taco in Los Angeles, but those were precursors he sold to create a Mexican specialty restaurant he would call Taco Bell.

Glen Bell would franchise Taco Bell across California in the 1960s and early 1970s. You couldn't miss the unique southwestern brick structures with the big bell on top. In addition to the hard-shell tacos, Taco Bell introduced the Bell Beefer, a sloppy-joe-like taco on a hamburger bun with cheese, lettuce, and tomato. The Beefer was later removed when Taco Bell went to a strict Tex-Mex lineup.

Taco Bell continued to grow, inspired by its inexpensive cuisine and great advertising. It's hard to pass up tasty food for under a buck. In the late 1990s Gidget the Chihuahua *quiero*-ed Taco Bell and made the brand a household name. And Taco Bell kept experimenting with its menu and innovating its product line. Taco Salad. Gorditas. The Crunchwrap Supreme. And, most recently, the Doritos Locos Tacos proved to be an enormous hit that has inspired a whole new line of tacos.

Get stuffed!

¡Yo Quiero Taco Bell!

I visited Taco Bell headquarters and spent some quality time with the CEO, and after cooking (playing around) in one of their innovation labs, it became clear to me why Taco Bell is so successful. Yes, they have quality ingredients and tons of unique combinations, but just as important, they have a good time with the brand. From sour cream guns to chips ending with *ito,* nothing is off-limits at Taco Bell, and that's how great fast food innnovation is made.

If you're going to sell your products for less than two bucks, you'd better sell a lot of them. And that's precisely what Taco Bell does. Two billion customers a year experience a fiesta when they order outside the bun.

And it's hard to find a favorite item at Taco Bell, because there are so many to choose from. Try everything. I guarantee you'll find a favorite quickly. And then Taco Bell will introduce five new items for you to try. That's why so many of us continue to "*quiero* Taco Bell."

Pure bliss—clad in a Taco Bell lab coat creating the next great taco.

Tim Hortons

		SPECIALTY ITEMS	SECRET MENU ITEMS
ESTABLISHED	1964	Coffee	Chai Tea Hot Chocolate
FOUNDER	Tim Horton	Apple Fritter	Toasted Sour Cream
GAME CHANGER	Tim Hortons Coffee	Boston Cream	Donut
FIRST LOCATION	Hamilton, Ontario	Chocolate Dip	
TOTAL LOCATIONS	Over 4,700	Sour Cream Glazed	
TRADEMARK	Timbits	Timbits	
MASCOT	Big Tim (Giant cup of coffee)	**SEASONAL SPECIALS**	**BEST**
		Roll Up the Rim to Win	Pastries (4)
CURRENT SLOGAN	Always Fresh	Jalapeño Biscuit	Coffee (3)
		Breakfast Sandwich	Sweepstakes (2)
CLASSIC SLOGAN	Always Fresh. Always Tim Hortons	**MUST HAVE**	
		The Coffee	
		Apple Fritter Donut	

Power of the Puck

In 1964 a National Hockey League all-star defenseman who played most of his career in Toronto decided to open a donut shop in Hamilton, Ontario. Soon after opening Tim Horton Donuts, Tim met Ron Joyce, who would eventually become his partner and help expand Tim Hortons all throughout Canada and parts of America. The shop originally sold two things—coffee and donuts—but Tim and crew got cre-

Always a welcome sign in the Great White North.

ative with their baked goods. The original Apple Fritter and Dutchie were huge hits in the 1960s and remain popular today.

In February of 1974 Tim Horton died in a tragic car crash on his way back from a hockey game at Maple Leaf Gardens, but his name lives on with the success of his restaurants. In the mid-1970s Tim Hortons introduced bite-sized donut holes called Timbits, which became the most popular item in the stores. These little gems have become part of the Canadian lexicon along with the place you bought them from, Timmy's. Today there are over 35 different varieties of Timbits available.

The menu expanded along with the franchise during the next two decades, but the staples of coffee and donuts remain at the core of Tim Hortons' success. The company went south of the border in 1984 in

Donut variety is not a problem up north.

Tonawanda, New York, and continues to grow throughout the United States. Tim Hortons changed the entire landscape of coffee and donut shops, a go-to place where the coffee and donuts are always fresh.

If you don't hail from Canada or the northern part of the United States and you're not a die-hard hockey fan, you might not know the name Tim Horton. Chances are you'll be finding out about him sooner rather than later as this successful franchise continues to grow.

Roll Up the Rim

Even up in the Great White North there's only so much you can do with a cup of coffee. In February of 1986 Tim Hortons unleashed its "Roll Up the Rim to Win" contest, with the big prize being a free box of Timbits. They haven't looked back since.

The game is simple and addicting—during the climax of

A nice warm cup of coffee from Timmy's.

the NHL season from March until May, special coffee cups are distributed. All you do is roll up the white rim on the top of the cup to see if you're a winner.

Over 31 million prizes are now distributed during the annual "Roll Up the Rim to Win" campaign. The times, and the prizes, have changed dramatically, but you can always catch customers rolling up the rims of their paper cups after finishing their drinks. Get rolling!

Wendy's

ESTABLISHED	1969	**SPECIALTY ITEMS**		**SECRET MENU ITEMS**	
FOUNDER	Dave Thomas	Baconator		Barnyard	
GAME CHANGER	Square Patties	Frosty		Big Bacon Classic	
		Single, Double, or Triple		Meat Cube (or Grand	
		Double Stack		Slam)	
FIRST LOCATION	Columbus, Ohio	Baked Potato		**BEST**	
TOTAL LOCATIONS	Over 6,500			Burgers (3)—*Double*	
TRADEMARK	Wendy			Milkshakes (5)—*Frosty*	
MASCOT	Wendy (in pigtails)			Ice (5)	
CURRENT SLOGAN	Now That's Better	**SEASONAL SPECIALS**		Chili (5)	
		Pretzel Bacon		Straws (4)	
		Cheeseburger		Drive-Thrus (1)	
		Ciabatta Bacon		Slogans (1)—*Where's the*	
		Cheeseburger		*Beef?*	
CLASSIC SLOGAN	Where's the Beef?	**MUST HAVE**		Ad Campaigns (4)	
		Frosty		Toy Collectibles (4)	
		Any Burger		OVERALL (3)	

Old Fashioned Hamburgers

If anyone deserves a knighthood for his or her contribution to fast food, right at the top of my list would be Dave Thomas. When he opened his first Wendy's Old Fashioned Hamburgers restaurant on November 15, 1969, in Columbus, Ohio, Dave was more than ready. He had worked with Colonel Sanders at Kentucky Fried Chicken in the 1950s, making invaluable suggestions like the bucket to keep the chicken crisp. When Dave opened his own burger place named for his fourth child, Wendy, square patties were the first of his many unique fast food innovations.

The very next year, Dave opened a second location in Columbus with a dedicated drive-thru window that had its own grill, beverage, and sandwich station. This modern-day pick-up station was the first of its kind, and fast food

Dave Thomas, a slam-dunk first-ballot fast food hall of famer.

restaurants still use Dave's system today. Instead of a shake, a thick, straw-proof Frosty (first chocolate, then vanilla) was available for dessert. In the late 1970s Wendy's introduced a salad bar and baked potato well before the push for healthy options began to happen.

Wendy's advertising couldn't be missed in the 1980s. Legendary campaigns such as "Where's the Beef?" gained a national cultlike following. All of a sudden, Wendy's was a real player in the 1-2 burger world of McDonald's and Burger King. Wendy's took advantage of the gem they had in Dave, as he appeared as the down-home spokesperson in EVERY advertisement for the company throughout the 1990s.

Although Dave passed away in 2002, Wendy's is number three behind McDonald's and Burger King in total locations and has continued to grow and please customers throughout the world.

Quality Is Our Recipe

Year after year, Wendy's is renowned for having the best drive-thru in the business. I got to work at a Wendy's drive-thru, and I can tell you firsthand how or-

Wendy's prides itself on its "Old Fashioned Hamburgers."

ganized it is. Once you start giving your order, the entire drive-thru staff, who are listening on headsets, begin to assemble your meal. When you pull around, a team has put your meal together in an orchestrated manner to keep you moving quickly and coming back for more.

Wendy's has never been afraid to shake things up in our fast food universe. The square patties have always been a hit, and the Baconator took Wendy's burgers to the next level. I love how every squeezable topping placed on your burger is in a W shape as the patties stack up.

Whether I'm at the counter or the drive-thru, I can always depend on the quality of a Wendy's meal. It's exactly what Dave Thomas wanted, and I'm happy to oblige with my many visits to his old fashioned hamburger restaurant.

WHAT YOU CRAVE.

ESTABLISHED	1921	SPECIALTY ITEMS		SECRET MENU ITEMS	
FOUNDER	Billy Ingram	The Original Slider		Bacon Crumbles	
GAME CHANGER	Sliders	Crave Case		Harold and Kumar's	
FIRST LOCATION	Wichita, Kansas	Castle Pack		Order	
TOTAL LOCATIONS	Over 400	Dessert on a Stick		Loaded Fries	
TRADEMARK	The Castle			Surf and Turf Slider	
MASCOT					
		SEASONAL SPECIALS			
CURRENT SLOGAN	What You Crave	Love Castle		BEST	
		Grilled Chicken Sliders			
CLASSIC SLOGAN	Buy 'Em by The Sack	MUST HAVE			
		Slider			

King of His Castle

In 1921 Billy Ingram sold some hamburgers out of the window of a little shack in Wichita, Kansas, and made a profit of $3.75. The first brick of White Castle had been laid. Americans were hesitant to eat ground beef after reading Upton Sinclair's *The Jungle,* an exposé about the unsanitary processing of meat, so when Ingram opened his first restaurant with cook Walt Anderson, it was all porcelain enamel to

The original Castle—buy 'em by the sack!

evoke cleanliness and looked like a white castle. That name stuck, and the first fast food hamburger restaurant chain was born.

White Castle's square hamburgers, known as sliders, were placed on an Anderson invention known as the hamburger bun. Now, *that's* innovation! Cooked on a grill with fresh onions, the bun was placed on top of the slider to keep the juices in as steam permeated the bun. In the 1950s, five holes were added in the patty to facilitate quicker cooking. Once cooked, a pickle was added and the slider, which is still cooked this way today, was complete. All condiments were to be added by the customer, a move I hold in the highest regard.

Billy Ingram bought out his partner in 1933 and moved the Castle headquarters to Columbus, Ohio. White Castle is not franchised, as the company has always remained in the Ingram family. The country continues to crave White Castle, where you can buy your burgers by the sack. A Cravers Hall of Fame was created in 2001 where White Castle fans are inducted based on their stories of slider dedication. When it comes to what you crave, no matter what time of the day or night, the answer is always White Castle.

The most influential burger in American history— the White Castle slider.

What You Crave

White Castle has the best sense of humor of any fast food chain. They have no problem being the butt of the joke, or being in on the joke. Harold and Kumar are not only welcome visitors, they are also honorary Cravers.

Every year on Valentine's Day, White Castle transforms into Love Castle. A maître d' is there to welcome you, red or white cloths and candles are on your table, and a special menu is prepared for February 14. Reservations must be made well in advance for the best romantic getaway any fast food couple could ask for.

Thirty sliders—to go.

And at the Castle, you don't just eat one slider. The Crave Case is one of the greatest inventions in fast food history. Thirty sliders, which is the exact amount of burgers that can be grilled at a single time, slide right in to this portable container so you can transport the crave to anyone. If you're feeling even more hungry, a Crave Crate of 100 sliders is your option. White Castle knows its customers.

The
REGIONALS

		SPECIALTY ITEMS	SECRET MENU ITEMS
ESTABLISHED	1963	Double Header	
FOUNDERS	The Vultaggio Family	Double Double	
GAME CHANGER	Double Header	Franks	
FIRST LOCATION	Massapequa, New York		
TOTAL LOCATIONS	1		
TRADEMARK	Timelessness		
MASCOT		SEASONAL SPECIALS	
CURRENT SLOGAN	Only One Original		BEST
	All-American		
CLASSIC SLOGAN		MUST HAVE	
		Double Header	
		Fries	
		Strawberry Shake	

The Pride of Massapequa

All American Drive-In is a throwback in every sense of the word, and that's the highest compliment that I can give this fast food institution. In 1963 the Vultaggio family opened its one and only location, in Massapequa, New York. That's the childhood home of Jerry Seinfeld and Alec Baldwin out on Long Island for you

My favorite thriving hamburger drive-in.

non–East Coasters. And you can still find the Vultaggios on Merrick Road in Massapequa, using their original recipes to make great burgers, fries, and shakes.

There is no drive-thru at All American Drive-In. There is no indoor seating. There are a handful of tables out front. In other words, your table is your car. No machines take or make your order, people do. And the menu is straightforward and simple. Looking for condiments? You're in the wrong place. Burger options are simple—cheese or no cheese. This is one classic burger joint.

Love the old-school All American menu.

All American bleeds nostalgia inside and out, from its red, white, and blue packaging to the Burgers/Franks neon sign atop the restaurant. All burgers are individually wrapped in foil to ensure they stay hot and fresh. As you wait in line, which moves quickly, until your number gets called, you're surrounded by others who are all in the know.

All American doesn't advertise. It thrives on word of mouth. It has been that way for over fifty years, and if I can help it, it will remain unchanged for fifty more.

Long Island's Only Hamburger Drive-In

All American is my favorite burger place on Long Island. It is one of a kind. I adore its simplicity, the nostalgic feel, and, of course, the food. My standard order is two Double Headers, two fries, and a strawberry shake. And even my car is excited when I return with this meal . . . trust me, I can tell.

But the real magic of All American is the people who work there and the customers you wait with. Local students work the registers and the grills. There are tons of kids with their parents after a game they've just won or lost. First dates, grandparents with their grandkids, and truckers or repairmen are all just waiting their turn. No one wants a drive-thru, or cares if they ever build one. Every town should really have a place like this.

All burgers are individually wrapped in foil to keep them toasty warm.

All American seems like it's out of a movie. And although they refer to an All American Burger in *Fast Times at Ridgemont High,* I can assure you that this Massapequa, New York, location is very real. I hope it never changes. Be sure to stop there before you head over to my house if you want me to invite you in.

BRAUM'S®

ESTABLISHED	1933	**SPECIALTY ITEMS**		**SECRET MENU ITEMS**	
FOUNDERS	Henry & Bill Braum	Peppermint Ice Cream			
GAME CHANGER	Vertical Integration	Butter Brickle Ice Cream			
FIRST LOCATION	Emporia, Kansas	All Fruit Banana Split			
TOTAL LOCATIONS	Over 275	Famous Crinkle Cut			
TRADEMARK	Fresh Milk	French Fries			
		Bag of Burgers			
MASCOT					
CURRENT SLOGAN	Braum's Makes Everything	**SEASONAL SPECIALS**			
	Better	Pecan Caramel		**BEST**	
		Cinnamon Crumb Cake		Ice Cream (5)	
		Sundae			
		Gingerbread Ice Cream			
CLASSIC SLOGAN		**MUST HAVE**			
		Turtle Sundae			
		Chocolate Chip Ice Cream			

Down on the Farm

In the 1930s Henry Braum began processing butter and milk on his farm in Emporia, Kansas. A few years later, he included ice cream made from his cows' fresh milk. His son, Bill, learned the business as he grew up, and in the 1950s father and son developed a chain of ice cream stores called Peter Pan Ice Cream, named after a local park and not Sandy Duncan's most famous role.

In 1967 Bill sold Peter Pan to a wholesaler, but not his herd and processing plant. The Braums couldn't sell ice cream in Kansas for ten years as a condition of the sale, so Bill and his wife, Mary, opened Braum's Ice Cream and Dairy Store in Oklahoma City. The largest dairy herd in Kansas was driven to Tuttle, Oklahoma, in the mid-1970s, and Braum's has been churning out amazing dairy products ever since.

I'm a Turtle Sundae.

Braum's is the only major ice cream maker in the U.S. that milks its own cows. Its dairy is one of the largest in the world, milking 1,600 cows per hour. When you taste the ice cream, you immediately recognize the freshness.

Braum's products come from their own farms, which guarantees quality and freshness. All Braum's stores are located within a 300-mile radius of Tuttle. Product deliveries occur seven days a week, and whether it's a burger or an ice cream cone, you can taste the difference. The Braum family has always believed that if you want something done right, you do it yourself. And we are all the better for it.

All in One

I had heard about Braum's, and when I was traveling through Oklahoma I spotted that neon ice cream cone. I was thrown a bit since there was a grocery, burger place, and ice cream stand all in one store, but I had to give it a try. What a combination: burger, fries, and chocolate chip ice cream that all tasted homemade.

Braum's fresh-from-the-cow ice cream is tough to beat. The standard flavors are available, but there's also Peppermint, Egg Nog, Butter Brickle, and other concoctions. Braum's helpings are always generous, and their shakes, sundaes, and mixes are simply delicious.

ESTABLISHED	1961	SPECIALTY ITEMS	SECRET MENU ITEMS
FOUNDER	George Propstra	Pepper Bacon Cheeseburger	All Banana Milkshake
GAME CHANGER	Progressive Burgers	Tillamook Cheeseburger	All Toppings Burger
FIRST LOCATION	Vancouver, Washington	Northwest Cherry	Protein Platter
TOTAL LOCATIONS	Over 40	Chocolate Shake	
TRADEMARK	Tillamook Cheese	Mocha Perk Milkshake	
MASCOT	Melvin Elk	SEASONAL SPECIALS	
CURRENT SLOGAN	Fresh Local Sustainable	Pumpkin Milkshake	BEST
		Fresh Strawberry Lemonade	
		Sweet Potato Fries	
		Portobello Burger	
CLASSIC SLOGAN	Serve with Love	MUST HAVE	
		Pepper Bacon Cheeseburger	

Born in Vancouver

In 1961, George Propstra, the son of a Dutch immigrant, opened Burgerville USA in Vancouver, Washington. George's father, Jacob, founded the Holland Creamery (also in Vancouver, Washington), and George took his father's lessons to heart—always serve fresh food with locally sourced ingredients, and don't forget your roots.

Burgerville operates under this mantra today, as they are committed to local businesses, farms, and producers. They practice what they preach.

At the original Burgerville, customers ordered from an outside window and all of the food was "to go." It offered regular burgers for 19 cents, and Colossal Burgers for 39 cents.

Burgerville was a local hit and began to grow, slowly but steadily. George's dry-humor television ads helped Burgerville achieve a cultlike status in Washington and Oregon, battling the national competitors with its local, fresh food. Burgerville was the place for Tillamook cheeseburgers and Walla Walla onion rings, and locals couldn't get enough.

The Pepper Bacon Cheeseburger (with Tillamook Cheddar cheese)

Burgerville has expanded to over 40 restaurants while continuing to be a company with a conscience. By staying committed to local merchants and focusing on doing right by its local customers, you feel a sense of civic pride walking into Burgerville. Not only do you get to choose from a unique menu and support the local economy when ordering here, you also feel like you're part of something special.

Season's Greetings

The menu at Burgerville is always changing, and that's a good thing. Burgerville provides a seasonal menu with different offerings on a monthly basis to complement its regular staples. Order a

The first Burgerville, in Vancouver, Washington.

Pumpkin Milkshake in the fall or Fresh Strawberry Lemonade in the spring. This manner of change provides an air of mystery and sweet anticipation. Who knows what will be on the menu next month or next year? The only constant is the Burgerville Original Spread, the secret sauce that accentuates just about everything you eat here.

A frequent guest on the radio show I work on is an employee of Burgerville, so when I found myself in Portland I had to drop by and experience the place for myself. I felt proud supporting the local economy as I scarfed down my burger, fries, and Strawberry Splash Milkshake (hold the OJ). I love fast food chains where you can feel the community spirit, and Burgerville certainly qualifies.

Burgerville's secret ingredient—the spread.

Cafe Rio
MEXICAN GRILL®

		SECRET MENU ITEMS
ESTABLISHED	1997	**SPECIALTY ITEMS**
FOUNDERS	Steve & Patricia Stanley	Enchilada Style Burrito
GAME CHANGER	Rio Grande Mexican	Taco Meal
FIRST LOCATION	St. George, Utah	Tortilla Soup
TOTAL LOCATIONS	Over 60	Nachos
TRADEMARK	The Comal	Sweet Pork Barbacoa
MASCOT		**SEASONAL SPECIALS**
CURRENT SLOGAN		Chile Rellenos
		Coconut Shrimp Tacos
CLASSIC SLOGAN	Make Every Meal a Masterpiece	**MUST HAVE**
		Cafe Rio Burrito

SPECIALTY ITEMS
Enchilada Style Burrito
Taco Meal
Tortilla Soup
Nachos
Sweet Pork Barbacoa

SEASONAL SPECIALS
Chile Rellenos
Coconut Shrimp Tacos

MUST HAVE
Cafe Rio Burrito

SECRET MENU ITEMS

BEST

Southern Utah Mexican Food

In 1997 Steve and Patricia Stanley were busy creating Mexican food in the style of Northern Mexico's Rio Grande, South Texas, and New Mexico. They opened their first Cafe Rio in St. George, Utah, and the restaurant was an immediate smash. The Stanleys opened six locations in Utah, making fresh Mexican meals every day from scratch. Bob Nilsen liked what he saw, and in 2004 he bought the restaurants and expanded the brand outside of the Beehive State (yes, Utah's state nickname is the Beehive State).

You can't miss Cafe Rio in Park City, Utah.

The secret to Cafe Rio's success in a crowded Mexican food field is its hand-made meals. Hundreds of tortillas are hand rolled each day, thousands of limes are squeezed, all avocados are hand scooped, and there aren't any microwaves or freezers in sight. Nothing is premade—everything is fresh. Olé!

And at the center of every Cafe Rio operation is the Comal, which you cannot miss upon entering the restaurant. The Comal is a huge round cooking surface that is extremely hot and where you'll find all of those fresh tortillas baking. You can't help but be mesmerized by this magical tortilla spinner, and we all benefit from the delicious results that it generates.

Cafe Rio continues to expand throughout the Southwest, because customers want fresh Mexican food with a little kick. The menu is straightforward and simple with

Gather 'round the Cafe Rio Comal.

burritos, enchiladas, tacos, and tostadas. As long as you can taste the difference, Cafe Rio will continue to grow and please its customers well beyond that tiny town in southern Utah.

The Rio Grande

The fasting-growing sector of the fast food business is Mexican food. Plenty of these restaurants are appearing with names that I struggle to pronounce, but this cuisine is adding a welcome game changer to the mix—fresh ingredients.

Cafe Rio has capitalized on this trend by preparing every meal fresh on a daily basis. A lot of cost, time, and people go into this, but the payoff is loyal customers who get to sample freshly made food from an open kitchen.

All Cafe Rio locations have daily specials where the cooks mess with the ingredients to come up with some delicious concoctions. Maria's Enchiladas, Yolanda's Tamales, and Coconut Shrimp Tacos are just a few of their unique treats.

Free Meal Fridays and Trade It Tuesdays have also become staples at Cafe Rio. Free Meal Fridays are

A fresh Cafe Rio burrito.

self-explanatory when they pop up on the calendar. On Tuesdays, though, customers offer to trade something, anything, for a meal. People, pets, or Nickelback CDs (yes, really) are not allowed to be offered, but most everything else is fair game. An attitude like this coupled with fresh food is helping build Cafe Rio into a formidable player in the world of Mexican food. And they've started to come east . . . you've been warned.

		SPECIALTY ITEMS	SECRET MENU ITEMS
ESTABLISHED	1976	The Bobbie	
FOUNDERS	Lois & Alan Margolet	The Capastrami	
GAME CHANGER	The Bobbie	Cole Turkey	
FIRST LOCATION	Wilmington, Delaware	Slaw Be Jo	
TOTAL LOCATIONS	Over 100		
TRADEMARK	The Bobbie		
MASCOT	Robert Cole Turkey	**SEASONAL SPECIALS**	
CURRENT SLOGAN	Extraordinary Food for Those Unwilling to Settle	Firecracker Spicy Turkey Sub	**BEST** Sandwiches—*The Bobbie*
CLASSIC SLOGAN	Share Our Passion—One Sandwich at a Time!	**MUST HAVE** The Bobbie	

A Turkey a Day

Lois Margolet grew up in the Little Italy neighborhood of Wilmington, Delaware. It was her lifelong dream to open her own sandwich shop, but there was plenty of local competition. You couldn't walk half a block in Little Italy without running into a sandwich shop, but that didn't deter Lois. She quit her job in 1976, borrowed some money, and bought a boarded-up building on North Union Street in Wilmington where the original Capriotti's Sandwich Shop, which she opened with her brother Alan, still stands.

The original Capriotti's in Wilmington, Delaware.

The shop is named after Lois and Alan's grandfather, Philip Capriotti, who loved to cook for his grandkids. Lois had a unique idea—capture the heart of real turkey lovers. This meant roasting whole fresh turkeys overnight, a completely novel concept in her Italian land of sandwich shops. And it worked. Word of mouth began to spread that you had to get a turkey sandwich from Capriotti's, and one turkey per night quickly became ten to twelve.

The Capastrami

Ten years later, Lois and Alan partnered with Diane Rizzo and opened additional shops in Delaware. Their signature sandwiches, like The Bobbie—aka Thanksgiving on a roll—and other specialty sandwiches quickly expanded the brand. Family members were offered franchises, and as demand grew, others were brought into the fold to carry on their sandwich shop tradition.

Capriotti's continues to grow and opened its 100th restaurant in 2014. If they manage to keep those signature sandwiches fresh and warm, their growth has no end in sight.

What About Bobbie

The must-have. Every restaurant strives for this. When it comes to sandwiches at Capriotti's, the must-have is The Bobbie.

Capriotti's has won countless awards for its sandwich making, but none of its offerings is more popular than The Bobbie: a sub consisting of turkey, cranberry sauce, stuffing, and mayonnaise.

The Bobbie is an example of how unique Capriotti's has always been in the world of subs. There are plenty of standard subs and a great-tasting cheese steak on the menu, but Cap's Specials are sandwiches you can find only at Capriotti's. The Capastrami, which is hot pastrami, Swiss cheese, Russian dressing, and coleslaw, has become a favorite. And every sandwich is made to order.

The award-winning Bobbie

The sub market is a tough one to crack, but no more difficult than when Lois Margolet started out in that Little Italy neighborhood in Wilmington. If you have a unique product that you can consistently deliver, you will stand out. Having one of the best-tasting sandwiches in America doesn't hurt either.

ESTABLISHED	1941	SPECIALTY ITEMS	SECRET MENU ITEMS
FOUNDERS	Carl & Margaret Karcher	Western Bacon Cheeseburger	
GAME CHANGER	Big Charbroiled Burgers	Famous Star	
FIRST LOCATION	Los Angeles, California	Double Philly	
TOTAL LOCATIONS	Over 1,400	Cheesesteak Burger	
TRADEMARK	Six Dollar Burger	Crisscut Fries	
		Fried Zucchini	
MASCOT	Happy Star	SEASONAL SPECIALS	
CURRENT SLOGAN	Eat Like You Mean It	Philly Cheesesteak Burger	BEST
		Buffalo Blue Cheese Burger	
CLASSIC SLOGAN	If It Doesn't Get All Over the Place, It Doesn't Belong in Your Face	MUST HAVE Double Western Bacon Cheeseburger Oreo Milkshake	

No Drive-In, No Problem

In 1941 Carl Karcher and his wife, Margaret, borrowed $311 on their Plymouth, emptied their savings account of $15, and purchased a hot dog cart in Los Angeles. One cart quickly turned into four, and in less than five years Carl's Drive-In BBQ opened with hamburgers on its menu. As the brand grew, smaller-size restaurants without drive-ins were opened, and to distinguish the smaller space these were aptly named Carl's Jr., which was all about quick service.

In the 1950s and 1960s, Carl's Jr. added drive-thrus for on-the-go California customers and carpeted dining rooms inside with music. It was easy to spot a Carl's Jr. with the Happy Star logo smiling down at you as you drove up. Carl's Jr. always prided itself on big burgers, and in the 1980s they introduced a cult classic—the Western Bacon Cheeseburger. This is the burger template that Carl's Jr. continues to build upon as the franchise constantly creates new burger combinations for customers to try.

Over the next two decades, even more notable than Carl's Jr. burgers were its ads, which are clearly targeted to young, hungry guys. Gorgeous models would gorge on big burgers, allowing the condiments to land wherever they may. The Happy Star lived its motto of "If It Doesn't Get All Over the Place, It Doesn't Belong in Your Face."

Carl's Jr. has partnered with different restaurants as it has continued to grow. On the West Coast, Green Burrito offers Mexican food to go along with the Happy Star. And on the East Coast, Hardee's restaurants share the Star and its menu. So if you spot that smiling star, you know what you're in for every time.

Six Bucks

Carl's Jr. has always offered large burgers plus a variety of combinations to choose from. They have the standard configurations, but are willing to try practically anything to keep things fresh at the Happy Star.

This experimentation was buoyed by the early success of the Western Bacon Cheeseburger, which is still popular decades later. The Philly Cheesesteak and Buffalo Blue Cheese are two examples of where Carl's is willing to go.

In the competitive California burger market, size *does* matter. Carl's Jr. Six Dollar Burger is a sit-down-restaurant type of burger offered at a fast food place. You can barely fit the burger in your mouth, which is just fine by me.

Carl's pulls no punches with its burgers or its ads. Women in bikinis eating gigantic burgers appeal to a certain demographic. And you don't have to be a perfect 10 to enjoy a Six Dollar Burger.

This is what a Six Dollar Burger looks like.

Carvel®

ESTABLISHED	1934	SPECIALTY ITEMS		SECRET MENU ITEMS	
FOUNDER	Tom Carvel	Flying Saucer		Mixed-In Crunchies	
GAME CHANGER	A Flat Tire	Brown Bonnet			
FIRST LOCATION	Hartsdale, New York	Cookie Puss			
TOTAL LOCATIONS	Over 400	Fudgie the Whale			
TRADEMARK	Flying Saucer	Carvelanche			
		Crunchies			
MASCOT	Fudgie the Whale	**SEASONAL SPECIALS**			
CURRENT SLOGAN	America's Freshest	Pumpkin		**BEST**	
	Ice Cream	Egg Nog		Ice Cream (4)	
		Peppermint			
		Swiss Miss			
CLASSIC SLOGAN	It's What Happy Tastes Like	**MUST HAVE**			
		Crunchies			
		Flying Saucer			
		Vanilla/Chocolate Twist			

A Serendipitous Flat Tire

Uttering the name Tom Carvel will bring a smile to the face of anyone who grew up in the New York metropolitan area. In 1929 Tom began selling ice cream and custard out of his very own truck, with some success. Five years later, Tom's truck got a flat in Hartsdale, New York, but the softening dessert didn't stop passersby from ordering the sweet treat. Tom wisely realized that people loved this softer, melting product, and his soft-serve ice cream was born. Tom opened his first ice cream shop right where his truck had broken down, and this Carvel store would change the industry forever.

Tom Carvel always innovated as his store grew in popularity. He invented his own freezer, the Custard King, to preserve his soft-serve delights. In 1951 Carvel introduced the Flying Saucer, which consists of soft-serve ice cream sandwiched between two large, soft cookies. Carvel also offered the Brown Bonnet, which is vanilla soft-serve ice cream dipped in hardening chocolate. Sprinkles are an option, but chocolate crunchies (small pieces of chocolate wafer cake) are unique to Carvel.

The famous Fudgie the Whale.

Carvel ice cream has always been delicious, but it is their cakes (and their wacky names) that really set this franchise apart. The two most iconic Carvel cakes are Fudgie the Whale (for a "whale of a dad" on Father's Day), and Cookie Puss (an ice cream face that defies description). The vanilla and chocolate ice cream bordered by chocolate crunchies is irresistible to kids of all ages, including yours truly.

Although Tom took his product very seriously, Carvel has always been about fun. Since 1936 Carvel has offered a "Buy One Get One Free" promotion, and everyone knows "Wednesday Is Sundae at Carvel." Carvel franchised over the years and expanded to different cities, mostly in the Northeast and Florida. The product list has grown, but nothing beats a Chocolate/Vanilla twist with crunchies in the middle and on top from your friendly neighborhood Carvel store.

The Voice of Soft Ice Cream

om Carvel's genius wasn't limited to ice cream invention—he was a master marketer who accidentally became a celebrity. Rumor has it that in the mid-1950s, Tom heard a radio ad that failed to give the location of a Carvel shop. So Tom went down to the station and did the ad himself in his gravelly, friendly voice, which clearly stood out.

So Tom continued to narrate Carvel ads over the next few decades, and if there was a Carvel in your area, you couldn't get enough of the guy. Carvel ads were extremely unsophisticated and most of his reads were completely unrehearsed. The hokey names and lack of production appealed to most people, and it didn't hurt that the ice cream was delicious.

And, by the way, do not come to Carvel with me if you are going to order traditional hand-dipped ice cream. That's like getting a

Carvel makes everyone smile, including my better half, Debbie.

burger at Nathan's. Carvel is all about the soft serve, cup or cone. Make sure to mix in crunchies (instead of sprinkles) for a delicious treat. If there is no store in your area, sample their football ice cream cake, which is coated with crunchies, from your supermarket's frozen section. The name isn't as catchy as Cookie Puss, but you won't find a more delicious ice cream cake anyplace else.

Culver's

ESTABLISHED	1984	SPECIALTY ITEMS	SECRET MENU ITEMS
FOUNDERS	Craig & Lea Culver	ButterBurger	Ultimate Grilled Cheese
GAME CHANGER	Frozen Custard	Concrete Mixer	Veggie Burger
FIRST LOCATION	Sauk City, Wisconsin	Concrete Cake	
		Flavor of the Day	
TOTAL LOCATIONS	Over 500	Cheese Curds	
TRADEMARK	ButterBurger		
MASCOT	Scoopie	SEASONAL SPECIALS	
CURRENT SLOGAN	Welcome to Delicious	Pumpkin Spice Shake	BEST
		Egg Nog Shake	Ice Cream—Frozen
CLASSIC SLOGAN	Taste How Much We Care	MUST HAVE	Custard
		Frozen Custard	Beverages (4)—Root
		Cheese Curds	Beer

The Cows Come Home

In 1984 the Culver family was faced with a unique opportunity in Sauk City, Wisconsin. An A&W property, which Craig Culver's parents had owned and sold back in 1968, was once again up for sale. Craig and his wife, Lea, jumped at the chance to reacquire this old property and put the Culver name on it. Craig wanted his new restaurant to feature two key items—his mom's homemade hamburgers and his favorite vacation treat, frozen custard. ButterBurgers and frozen custard would constitute Culver's Signature Combination.

Craig is the son of a Wisconsin farmer who knows customers can distinguish the difference in his products. Culver's prides itself on its freshness, whether it's a burger or frozen custard that you're after. Each sunrise brings a new frozen custard Flavor of the Day, and if you travel to another Culver's on the same day, you'll find a different flavor featured there.

You'll always find the Flavor of the Day on the Culver's sign.

ButterBurgers are exactly what they sound like—fresh beef on a buttered roll. The Signature Combination is still quite popular, but Culver's menu has expanded to offer a variety of treats to its customers. If you find yourself driving in the northern part of the Midwest and a big blue sign looms overhead, pull in for a ButterBurger and some frozen custard. You won't regret it.

On Wisconsin

My brother went to college at the University of Wisconsin, and on the long drive there he insisted that we stop at Culver's. I had heard of their

The ButterBurger

frozen custard, so I entered with sky-high expectations. Not only were they met, but they were exceeded. I also knew that I'd be visiting my brother again in Madison very soon.

Fresh product is the key to keeping franchises like Culver's thriving. You can truly recognize the difference in its frozen custard. When you dine at Culver's, it feels (and tastes) like a homemade meal from Mom's kitchen. And whether you take your food to go or stay right there, Culver's travels with you—and I mean that in a good way.

ESTABLISHED	1964	SPECIALTY ITEMS	SECRET MENU ITEMS
FOUNDER	Ed Hackbarth	Double Beef Classic Taco	Bun Taco
GAME CHANGER	Bean and Cheese Burrito	Crinkle Cut Fries	Go Bold
FIRST LOCATION	Yermo, California	Del Cheeseburger	Stoner Burrito
TOTAL LOCATIONS	Over 540	Fish Taco	
TRADEMARK	Hot Sauce	Chicken Soft Taco	
MASCOT	Del Taco Dan		
CURRENT SLOGAN	Unfreshing Believable	SEASONAL SPECIALS	BEST
		Turkey Tacos	
		Crispy Shrimp	
CLASSIC SLOGAN	Go Bold or Go Home	MUST HAVE	
		Chicken Soft Taco	
		Bean and Cheese Burrito	

Fresh and Inexpensive

For fifty years, Del Taco has been offering fresh made-to-order Mexican and American menu items at low, low prices. It all started in 1964 when Ed Hackbarth opened the first Del Taco in Southern California. Five other locations quickly debuted featuring Del Taco's unique combination of Mexican and American food. The fifth location, in Corona, California, was the chain's first to feature a drive-thru, more than a

Del Taco through the years—it operated a drive-thru well before McDonald's did, and note the old sun logo.

decade before McDonald's would do so. Burritos and burgers, tacos and fries, they were all available under one SoCal roof, and prices were always very low.

Del Taco really began to expand in the 1970s, with over 100 restaurants and adding the Bun Taco (a taco served on a hamburger bun instead of in a tortilla), quesadillas, and ice cream sundaes to its menu. Acquiring the Naugles restaurant chain in the 1980s increased Del Taco's size and geographic reach, and Del Taco began operating 24/7 to satisfy customer demand. Breakfast began to be served in 1983—well before the nationwide breakfast burrito craze.

Del Taco overhauled its look in the 1990s, changing its famous sun logo and classing up the existing restaurants in the chain. Del Taco grew in the Southwest and even has dabbled in Detroit, but Southern California has always been home.

The perfect side to a burger or burrito.

Mexican American

Del Taco knows that if it ain't broke, you don't fix it. Ed Hackbarth, the founder of Del Taco, can still be spotted working at his original location. The Del Cheeseburger and crinkle-cut fries on the Del Taco menu in 1964 reside on its menu today. It is this consistency that customers have come to know and love at Del Taco.

Daily fresh ingredients make the difference at Del Taco.

Hamburgers and burritos might seem like an odd combination, but Del Taco has provided a one-stop shop for either cuisine for fifty years. The company's menu includes classic Mexican dishes such as tacos, burritos, quesadillas, and nachos, as well as American favorites, including cheeseburgers, crinkle-cut fries, and shakes.

I love how Del Taco continues to offer Mexican and American items separately. This gives you endless combo opportunities—order a burger with a side of nachos, or wash down a burrito with a shake! You always have options at Del Taco.

Drive-In Restaurants

		SPECIALTY ITEMS	SECRET MENU ITEMS
ESTABLISHED	1954	Dick's Deluxe	
FOUNDERS	Dick Spady, Warren Ghormley, Tom Thomas	Dick's Special	
GAME CHANGER	19-Cent Burgers	Fries	
FIRST LOCATION	Wallingford, Washington	Shakes	
TOTAL LOCATIONS	6		
TRADEMARK	Dick's Deluxe		
MASCOT		**SEASONAL SPECIALS**	
CURRENT SLOGAN	Where Taste Has Been the Difference Since 1954		**BEST**
CLASSIC SLOGAN	Where Taste Is the Difference	**MUST HAVE**	
		Dick's Deluxe	
		Fries	
		Strawberry Shake	

Burgers in Seattle

In the 1950s, everyone was looking for a place to pull up in their cars to enjoy a burger, fries, and a shake. Twenty-nine-year old Dick Spady, along with Warren Ghormley and Tom Thomas, wanted to make that dream a reality in Seattle. Their goal was to serve fresh, quality food at low prices with instant service, but many were skeptical that 19-cent burgers could make a profit. They were wrong. In 1954 the first

Dick's Drive-In opened for business in Wallingford, right down the road from the University of Washington, and it has been serving burgers, fries, and shakes with very few changes for the past 60 years.

Every few years a new Dick's location would open in a nearby area, but success didn't lead to national franchising. Family came first, and the partners wanted to keep the business close by and have it grow in Seattle. That is why there are only 6 locations in the Seattle area, and they are all worth traveling to. And the menu has hardly changed in the 60 years Dick's has been serving burgers, fries, and shakes in Seattle.

In fact, the appeal of Dick's is how it *doesn't* change. They won't modify your order or add limited-time offers to the menu. What you see is what you get, and customers keep coming back for more.

The iconic sign in Wallingford, Washington.

Spare Change

There have been some changes to Dick's as time has progressed. In the late 1950s, separate lines for fries and burgers were eliminated, allowing customers to place a full order at the same window. In the early 1970s, the Dick's Special and Dick's

Deluxe were added to the cheeseburger and hamburger on the menu. Orange soda was also dropped and Diet Coke was added, and that pretty much wraps up all the changes that have been made since their opening in 1954.

The first time I traveled to Seattle, I had to get to Dick's. And it had to be in the original Wallingford location, because it seemed like the right thing to do. I pulled up and saw the iconic sign spinning around and knew I was in the right place. I felt like I was in the 1950s as I walked up to the window to order.

Dick's Deluxe—don't ask them to hold anything. They won't.

I was prepared. I knew Dick's didn't take any special orders, so I went with Dick's Deluxe, fries, and a strawberry shake. The price was right, the service was quick, and I was sitting on the hood of my car sampling Seattle's finest. I wouldn't have had it any other way.

I can only imagine the feeling that locals or former University of Washington students must get when going to Dick's. The world has changed, but Dick's really hasn't. That's what I call progress.

ESTABLISHED	1956	SPECIALTY ITEMS	SECRET MENU ITEMS
FOUNDERS	Harold & Jack Berkowitz	Big D Cheeseburger	
GAME CHANGER	Short Order Cooks	Big D Pastrami & Swiss	
FIRST LOCATION	Bridgeport, Connecticut	Big D Patty Melt	
TOTAL LOCATIONS	15	Long Dog	
TRADEMARK	Fresh Fast Food		
MASCOT		**SEASONAL SPECIALS**	
CURRENT SLOGAN	Fresh Food Served Fast	Big D Grilled Chicken Sandwich	BEST
CLASSIC SLOGAN	Fast Food Fresh	**MUST HAVE**	
		Big D Cheeseburger	

Fast Food, Diner-Style

Harold and Jack Berkowitz successfully opened diners throughout Connecticut, but both wondered if you could create a place that could compete with fast food by offering fresh food on the go. In 1956, the Berkowitzes decided to find out and opened the first Duchess restaurant, in Bridgeport, Connecticut. Short order cooks are the key to Duchess's success, making every meal on the menu a little more special. The cook has always been the most important person in any Duchess restaurant—everything is made from scratch to order, and it needs to be cooked in a hurry.

As Duchess expanded throughout Connecticut, it never abandoned its roots as a diner. It offers traditional burgers, dogs, fries, and shakes, but all of these can be fully customized since the food is made to order. More than 100 items have become mainstays on the menu beside the fast food staples. At Duchess, you're not limited as you pass through the drive-thru, and customers keep coming back to explore different options.

This Connecticut mainstay is beckoning you.

The Big D

When I was working on my VH1 Classic show *For What It's Worth,* our director, Jeff, knew of my love for fast food and casually asked me about "the Duchess." I had no idea what he was referring to. You should have seen his eyes pop out. He asked how it's possible that I've never had the Big D. I said I wasn't from Connecticut like he was, and in my travels through the state I never encountered a Duchess. This had to be remedied immediately.

Delicious Duchess Dogs.

When I learned about their short order cooking system, I couldn't believe it. I tested the Duchess by going through the drive-thru. There's no way they could quickly turn around a Big D Patty Melt, fries, and a chocolate shake, right? When I pulled around, my food was ready—and it was freshly made. The hot dogs are pretty great too.

The Big D. Yes, it's that good.

Duchess restaurants receive ingredients daily, sometimes six deliveries per day, so that limits the number of restaurants you can open if you don't want to sacrifice quality. And they don't. So next time you're cruising through Connecticut, keep your eyes peeled for "the D."

		SPECIALTY ITEMS	SECRET MENU ITEMS
ESTABLISHED	1975	Pollo Bowl	Skinless Chicken
FOUNDER	Juan Francisco Ochoa	Half Chicken Combo	
GAME CHANGER	Open Grill Chicken	Poblano Burrito	
FIRST LOCATION	Guasave, Mexico	Churros	
TOTAL LOCATIONS	Over 415		
TRADEMARK	Fire-Grilled Chicken		
MASCOT		**SEASONAL SPECIALS**	
CURRENT SLOGAN	Crazy You Can Taste	Roja Wet Burrito	**BEST**
		Avocado Bacon Tostada	Burritos (1)
CLASSIC SLOGAN	When You're Crazy for	**MUST HAVE**	
	Chicken	Ultimate Pollo Bowl	

The Crazy Chicken

The story of El Pollo Loco starts south of the border in the small town of Guasave on the Pacific coast of Mexico. No one could walk by the aroma emanating from the roadside chicken stand of Juan Francisco Ochoa cooking on an open grill. The chicken stand featured a family recipe for fresh marinated chicken fire-grilled to perfection. The stand's name was El Pollo Loco, which translates into The Crazy Chicken,

Crazy chicken from a Mexican stand built this.

and the local favorite began to spread throughout Northern Mexico over the next five years.

In 1980 El Pollo Loco crossed the border and arrived on Alvarado Street in Los Angeles with lines forming around the block to get a taste of this crazy chicken. Expansion continued as it did in Mexico, spreading all over the southwestern United States. Self-served salsa and guacamole accompanied a variety of dishes featuring the magical chicken. El Pollo Loco expanded its menu as well, adding new burritos and creating the world's largest, weighing two tons, in the mid-1990s.

In 1996 the Pollo Bowl became the most popular item at El Pollo Loco. Two new fresh-made salsas,

The fire-grilled chicken of El Pollo Loco.

avocado and pico de gallo, also came on the scene to accompany the house salsa. El Pollo Loco continues to grow, and you'd be crazy not to sample its fire-grilled chicken.

Crossing the Border

El Pollo Loco was tremendously popular in Mexico before it came to the United States in 1980. By 1983 Denny's had acquired the American restaurants of El Pollo Loco, as it realized how popular Mexican cuisine was becoming.

California is the battleground of Mexican fast food, and if you can make it there you can make it anywhere. The unique offering El Pollo Loco has is its chicken—which is marinated in Mexican herbs and spices that no one can match. Incorporating the chicken into different menu offerings is the easy part.

The legendary Pollo Bowl is a combination of chicken, Spanish rice, and pinto beans topped with onions, cilantro, and salsa—and it only has 10 grams of fat. This delicious low-calorie fast food option, and its many variations, was a game changer for El Pollo Loco and way ahead of its time. The Bowls made customers as passionate about chicken as El Pollo Loco is— and that's some crazy chicken.

The Pollo Bowl—crazy chicken.

ESTABLISHED	2005	SPECIALTY ITEMS		SECRET MENU ITEMS
FOUNDER	Hans Hess	Elevation Burger		BLT
GAME CHANGER	Organic Fast Food	Vertigo Burger		Paleo Burger
FIRST LOCATION	Falls Church, Virginia	Half the Guilt Burger		Thick and Rare Burger
TOTAL LOCATIONS	Nearly 100			
TRADEMARK	Vertigo Burger			
MASCOT		SEASONAL SPECIALS		
CURRENT SLOGAN	Ingredients Matter	Peppermint Indulgence		BEST
		Shake		
		Pumpkin Pie à la mode		
		Shake		
CLASSIC SLOGAN		MUST HAVE		
		Vertigo Burger		
		Any Shake		

It's All Organic

Hans Hess conceived Elevation Burger in 2002, and three years later he was opening his first restaurant. He and his wife, April, wanted a burger that not only was unique and tasted great but was also made from organic, sustainable, and fresh ingredients. Elevation Burger was quickly labeled the first organic burger joint, and

Even the outside of Elevation Burger feels organic.

the brand has taken off from there. The menu features burgers made with 100 percent grass-fed organic beef, fresh-cut fries cooked in olive oil, veggie burgers, and hand-blended milkshakes.

A standard order at Elevation Burger.

But don't make the mistake of thinking that you can't fill up on these organic delights. The Vertigo Burger, which is made with 3 to 10 patties, takes care of that issue head-on. Veggie burgers are kept separate from beef burgers, so there's no crossover on the grill. But if you're looking to dabble in both worlds, the Half the Guilt Burger is tailor-made, featuring one beef and one veggie patty.

Elevation Burger shakes are hand-blended, which guarantees freshness. As we all get more health conscious, Elevation Burger fills the need of a good-tasting, filling meal in an eco-friendly setting.

How High Can You Go?

I have to admit that I was suspicious when I first visited Elevation Burger, worried that this organic burger couldn't possibly taste good. After spending some quality time in the restaurant, I'm happy to report how displaced my initial fears were.

After being given an opportunity to help work the grill for a bit and sampling some of the cuisine, I was ready to create a Vertigo Burger. The suggested range for a Vertigo Burger is 3 to 10 patties, but I thought we could do better. So we made a 20-plus-patty burger, stacked it like the Leaning Tower of Pisa, and shared the result with all the lucky EB customers who were there.

That many patties might be a bit much for some, but it captures the spirit of Elevation Burger. Yes, they are extremely health conscious and are creating healthy fast food, but that doesn't keep them from stacking over 20 organic patties to make a ginormous burger. I'm still digesting that Vertigo Burger, but it did taste really good.

I'm on the left, helping to build the Vertigo Burger. Smart move to keep me back.

IN·N·OUT® BURGER

ESTABLISHED	1948	SPECIALTY ITEMS		SECRET MENU ITEMS	
FOUNDERS	Harry & Esther Snyder	Double-Double		3 x 3	
GAME CHANGER	Two-Way Speaker System	French Fries		4 x 4	
FIRST LOCATION	Baldwin Park, California	Shakes		Animal Style (Burger or	
TOTAL LOCATIONS	Over 300	The Secret Menu		Fries)	
TRADEMARK	Animal Style			Cheese Fries	
MASCOT				Double Meat	
		SEASONAL SPECIALS		Extra Large Shakes	
				Extra Toast	
				Flying Dutchman	
				Grilled Cheese	
				Neapolitan Shake	
				Protein Style	
				Well Done Fries	
CURRENT SLOGAN	Quality You Can Taste			BEST	
CLASSIC SLOGAN	No Delay	MUST HAVE		Burgers (1)—Double-	
		Double-Double		Double	
		Well Done Fries		Fries (3)	
		Neapolitan Shake		Secret Menus (1)	
				Uniforms (4)	
				OVERALL (2)	

West Coast Greatness

Harry Snyder and his wife, Esther, established the first In-N-Out Burger in Baldwin Park, California, in 1948. This was the first drive-thru hamburger stand in California that allowed customers to place their orders through a two-way speaker system. Harry chose fresh meat and ingredients by hand and cooked all day, and by night he built that groundbreaking two-way speaker system. The name on the sign told carhop customers what they were in for—an in-and-out burger experience.

My pearly gates.

In 1954 the In-N-Out Burger logo with its yellow arrow pointing at the store made its debut. "Animal Style" arrived in the early 1960s with a mustard-cooked patty, lettuce, tomato, pickles, grilled onions, and extra spread. After Harry enjoyed seeing *It's a Mad, Mad, Mad, Mad World,* a movie about a hunt for stolen cash, crossed palm trees were planted in front of locations, signifying the treasure to be found inside. Shakes arrived in the mid-1970s along with the first sit-down location, but all locations were based in California to ensure the delivery of fresh food.

Harry Snyder died in 1976, but the Snyder family has carried on his legacy as In-N-Out grew throughout California and crossed the border into Nevada. As In-N-Out has continued to expand in the Southwest after building a Texas processing plant, quality has always been a priority. Whether you're in Texas or Arizona, the In-N-Out experience is always the same—quality food and quality service. They will not expand beyond the range of their special food-processing plants, in order to ensure freshness at every location. As an East Coaster, I begrudgingly respect that.

My favorite West Coast sight to see.

From the paper hats to its secret menu, In-N-Out has always been a fun trip out for a meal. But it's the freshness of the meat, fries, and shakes that truly sets it apart from the competition. The menu is simple—hamburger, cheeseburger, or Double-Double. Fries. Shakes. And that's it. Its secret menu is legendary, with many variations on basic items (see my Secret Menu Item Dossier, page 265). In-N-Out Burger is a destination, and I pray one day they will bring their quality offerings back east.

My Must-Have Meal

I f I ever have the pleasure of traveling with you to Vegas or any city in California, be aware that when the plane lands we will be taking a detour before arriving at our eventual destination. My first stop is always In-N-Out Burger. Always. It's THAT good. And yes, I'm an obsessed East Coaster.

How obsessed? If you're my taxi driver, I will take you there. A Vegas cabbie and I sat down for a meal on my way to losing money at the Encore. If I rent a car and need directions, bank on me asking for a route that includes a stop at an In-N-Out.

There is not just one thing that makes In-N-Out so exceptional. It's EVERYTHING. The simple menu. The secret menu. The freshness of the burgers. The fries. The shakes. The service. It is the ultimate fast food package.

When I give my standard order of Double Meat, Well Done Fries, and an extra-large Neapolitan shake, the cashier just goes about

I tried to take the picture before finishing my In-N-Out meal. No luck.

his or her business, even though they're all secret menu items (naturally). No explanation needed. No questions asked. Strictly professional.

My only knock on In-N-Out is the "Not-So-Secret Menu" on its website. Let's keep the Secret Menu a secret, shall we? Wait a minute, I wrote a Secret Menu Item Dossier in this book. Never mind, I guess In-N-Out Burger is perfect after all. See you under the crossed palm trees in front.

ESTABLISHED	1953	SPECIALTY ITEMS		SECRET MENU ITEMS
FOUNDER	Jim Shafer	Double, Triple, Quad, or		
GAME CHANGER	The Blimpy Burger	Quint Blimpy Burger		
FIRST LOCATION	Ann Arbor, Michigan	Fries or Veggies from		
TOTAL LOCATIONS	1	the Fryer		
TRADEMARK	The Blimpy Burger			
MASCOT	Snow Bear	SEASONAL SPECIALS		
CURRENT SLOGAN				BEST
CLASSIC SLOGAN	Cheaper Than Food	MUST HAVE		Burgers—*Quad*
		Blimpy Burger		
		Anything from the Fryer		

Cheaper Than Food

Jim Shafer wasn't so crazy when he opened Krazy Jim's Blimpy Burger at 551 South Division Street in Ann Arbor, Michigan, back in 1953. This burger joint blended right into the campus of the University of Michigan. Blimpy's was a dive that cared about one thing and one thing only: great greasy burgers and fried sides that kept you coming back for more.

Blimpy's has served four generations of Ann Arborites with its unique cartoon-styled menu and strict set of rules. "Cheaper than food" has always been the restaurant's ironic motto. The furniture never changed in the old brick building located right on campus, and neither has the grill or what you can order. Blimpy addicts don't mind at all. In fact, we look forward to it.

A true work of art—the Blimpy menu.

Rich Magner, who worked at Blimpy's and designed the original logo, bought Blimpy Burger in 1992 and kept the dream alive. Each winter he sculpts gigantic snow bears in front of the store, which warm the heart of many freezing college students.

In 2013 the sixty-year-old building of Blimpy's was sold to the university (Magner did not own the land, just the restaurant), and the best burger place in Michigan was homeless. A crowdsourcing campaign sprung up, and all of those lifelong Blimpy addicts (including yours truly) put their money where their mouths were and saved the snow bears. A new Blimpy's opened in the summer of 2014 on South Ashley, and although the address is different, the spirit of Krazy Jim remains alive.

"*Something from the Fryer?*"

The Quad has found a new home in Ann Arbor—thank God.

I lived on the same street as Krazy Jim's when I was a student in Ann Arbor, so you can probably imagine how many trips I took there. It is a special place in so many ways. Little balls of meat are grilled into loose patties right in front of your eyes. Fries or veggies out of the fryer always taste fresh and hot.

Blimpy's felt like it never left the sixties with its scrawled sayings and loose vibe, but the ordering is very strict—Soup Nazi style. You begin your order by responding

That's me showing my daughter Emily how it's done at Blimpy's. Dad has plenty of experience.

to the standard question "Something from the fryer?", since those items take the longest to make. Then you choose your Blimpy size (Double, Triple, Quad, or Quint), what kind of roll (plain, onion, kaiser, etc.), and any grilled items you want on the burger. As the burger is grilled in front of your eyes, you decide on the cheese that you want (if any), and then condiments (wet ones first, then dry). That's the system. Keep the line moving. It doesn't vary, and if you don't know it, your life is in your own hands.

It's a shame that the original location was sold, but Rich Magner exemplifies the spirit and humor of Krazy Jim. The South Ashley location has that vibe (I've already been there twice), and I will be coming back for more.

ESTABLISHED	1932	SPECIALTY ITEMS	SECRET MENU ITEMS
FOUNDERS	Rody Davenport Jr. & J. Glenn Sherrill	Cheese Krystals	Quad Cheese
		Krystal Chiks	
GAME CHANGER	Square Burgers	Pups	
		Kryspers	
FIRST LOCATION	Chattanooga, Tennessee		
TOTAL LOCATIONS	Over 350		
TRADEMARK	The Krystal		
MASCOT	Krystal the Burger	SEASONAL SPECIALS	
CURRENT SLOGAN		Philly Cheese Krystal	BEST
		Nutter Butter Milkquake	Chili (3)
CLASSIC SLOGAN	Nothing Like It		Drive-Thrus (5)
		MUST HAVE	
		Krystal	
		Krystal Chiks	

Krystal with a K

The Great Depression doesn't seem like an ideal time to open up a new restaurant, but that's exactly what Rody Davenport Jr. and J. Glenn Sherrill did in Chattanooga, Tennessee, on October 24, 1932, with The Krystal. They bet on a clean restaurant with good service and low prices, and when their first customer ordered six

Krystals (as they named their mini burgers) and a cup of coffee for 35 cents, a southern fast food giant was born. Krystal is often likened to the Castle up north, with its small square burgers available by the sack and inexpensive pricing. The restaurant was clean as a crystal, but a *k* instead of a *c* in front added a memorable twist.

Krystal served its food and coffee on porcelain with the Krystal moniker proudly displayed. The menu has expanded over time while maintaining the same Krystal shape, offering Chiks (small chicken sandwiches), Pups (small hot dogs with chili and cheese), and Sunrisers (small breakfast sandwiches). Prices have always remained low, and customers have continued to load up on Krystals in bulk.

The famous Krystal burger.

Krystal also held the Krystal Square Off from 2004 to 2009, a competitive eating contest consuming, what else, Krystals. The world record is held by Joey Chestnut, who ate 103 Krystal burgers in 8 minutes in 2007 (Joey also holds the Nathan's hot dog eating record). Although the Square Off is long gone, it just goes to show that nobody can have just one Krystal.

Not the Castle

It's natural to compare Krystal to White Castle. Founding partner Rody Davenport Jr. visited White Castle before he decided to open Krystal in Chattanooga. The two franchises hardly overlap geographically in the United States, and there's definitely room for both.

The Krystal burger is a square hamburger slider with a steamed bun plus onions, pickles, and mustard. The mustard is the big difference between this and a White Castle slider, which contains ketchup instead. Other than that, the products

A cute little Chik.

are nearly identical, so if you have a craving and you're in the South, Krystal gets the job done.

The Krystal Chiks have also proven to be very popular since their introduction in 1998. These small chicken squares are quite yummy, and the more you eat, the merrier you become. Pups, which feel like pigs in a blanket on steroids, are also unique to Krystal and set them apart from the Castle.

Whether it's White Castle or Krystal, there will always be a special place in my heart (and stomach) for inexpensive, small sandwiches you just can't get enough of.

A HOLLYWOOD LEGEND SINCE 1939

		SPECIALTY ITEMS	SECRET MENU ITEMS	
ESTABLISHED	1939	Stretch Chili Cheese Dog		
FOUNDERS	Paul & Betty Pink	Guadalajara Dog		
GAME CHANGER	Chili Dog	Bacon Chili Cheese Dog		
FIRST LOCATION	Hollywood, California	Polish Dog		
TOTAL LOCATIONS	15	Rosie O'Donnell Dog		
TRADEMARK	Hollywood Star Hot Dogs	Martha Stewart Dog		
MASCOT		**SEASONAL SPECIALS**		
CURRENT SLOGAN	America's Top Hot Dog		**BEST**	
CLASSIC SLOGAN	A Hollywood Legend	**MUST HAVE**	Hot Dogs (2)	
	Since 1939	Stretch Chili Dog		

A Hollywood Legend

There's the Hollywood sign. There's the Chinese Theatre. And then there's Pink's. Paul Pink started selling hot dogs out of the pushcart he and his wife, Betty, bought in 1939 in the midst of the Great Depression. Pink's Chili Dogs, which were oversize hot dogs covered in mustard, onions, and thick chili, sold for 10 cents each in the "weeds" of Los Angeles at the corner of La Brea and Melrose. A few years later, Paul traded his hot dog wagon for a small building constructed on the spot where his

Pink's is built in the very spot where its original cart thrived.

pushcart had stood. And the hot dog stand built in 1946 hasn't changed very much since then.

Sure, the price has gone up during the past 68 years, but the quality of the hot dogs has never wavered. The hot dogs are huge, the toppings are generous, and the service is just as fast, with customers getting their orders in less than a minute. Pink's has always been a Hollywood hot spot, a place to be seen, and stars have made a point to eat at Pink's and lend their names to its menu. Customers are happy to wait at this Hollywood landmark, wondering which celebrity might show up for a hot dog. Pink's even has its own parking-lot attendant, proving that it is truly part of Hollywood.

Pink's famous Chili Cheese Dog.

Pink's offers all different types of hot dogs, but is best known for its chili dog. Variations include a stretch dog, which is 9 inches long, and combinations ranging from New York (sweet & saucy onions) to Chicago (mustard, relish, onions, tomatoes, lettuce) or Guadalajara (relish, onions, tomatoes, sour cream) to Polish (mustard, chili, onions). Pink's also has burgers, fries, onion rings, and desserts, but most people come for the dogs.

It's All in the Name

I was surprised by the variety on Pink's menu the first time I went there, but there was no way I was going to get anything besides a hot dog. I'm a purist that way. The first time I went to Pizza Hut, I ordered a pizza. At KFC, I got the FC. You get the drift.

The hot dog lives up to the hype, and so does the people watching. I mean, this *is* the place where Bruce Willis proposed to Demi Moore. Icons such as Orson Welles, Michael Jackson, and Marlon Brando frequented Pink's. And Pink's is wise to capitalize on its celebrity quotient by naming hot dogs after its visitors. Martha Stewart, Rosie O'Donnell, Huell Howser, and Ozzy Osbourne are but a few of Hollywood's finest who have a menu item named after them.

Pink's is well worth the wait.

But celebrity names only get you so far. You need to deliver on your product, and Pink's has done that with its dogs since 1939. If you're planning a trip to L.A., make sure Pink's is one of your stops. You never know who you'll see in line—maybe you'll even spot me.

PRIMANTI BROS.

ESTABLISHED	1933	SPECIALTY ITEMS	SECRET MENU ITEMS
FOUNDER	Joe Primanti	Almost Famous	
GAME CHANGER	Almost Famous Sandwich	Sandwich	
FIRST LOCATION	Pittsburgh, Pennsylvania	The Pitts-burger	
TOTAL LOCATIONS	20	Smallman Street Fries	
TRADEMARK	Almost Famous Sandwich		
MASCOT			
CURRENT SLOGAN		SEASONAL SPECIALS	
		Penguins Game Time	BEST
		Menu	Sandwiches (2)—*Almost*
		Pizza Feast	*Famous*
CLASSIC SLOGAN	A Pittsburgh Tradition for	MUST HAVE	
	Over 70 Years	Almost Famous	
		Sandwich	

A One of a Kind Sandwich

It is nearly impossible to make a sandwich that is truly one of a kind, but that's exactly what Primanti Bros. (short for Brothers) has been doing since 1933. Joe Primanti opened a cart selling sandwiches to truckers traveling through Pittsburgh's Strip District at all hours of the night. His success led to opening a storefront that remained open from 3 a.m. to 3 p.m., satisfying Pittsburgh truckers and shift workers.

The first Primanti Bros. in 1933.

One winter, a trucker brought in a load of potatoes, which Joe fried and decided to put INSIDE the sandwich. History was made, and Primanti Bros. has been re-creating that feat ever since.

The Almost Famous Sandwich is a concoction like no other. Your meat of choice is topped with fresh-cut fries, provolone cheese, tomatoes, and house-made cole-slaw sandwiched between two slices of Italian bread. Yes, French fries are a topping—talk about a one-stop shop. Primanti Bros. also has great wings, pizza, and beer, but most customers are there for the sandwich.

Primanti Bros. expanded from that original Strip District location to 17 in the Pittsburgh area, and three more down in Florida. The restaurants are laid back and

The famous Almost Famous Sandwich

typically filled with Pittsburgh sports fans (not a requirement, but recommended), and they all offer the Almost Famous Sandwich. So when you go to Primanti Bros. for the first time, that sandwich is all you need to order. It will certainly fill you up.

Steel, Sports, and Sandwiches

Pittsburgh was long known for its steel mills and great sports teams, but when it came to food there was always one signature item to be had. Many cities have that one spot or item you *must* eat while you're there. Primanti Bros. Almost Famous Sandwich (which is pretty famous these days) is that item. And Primanti Bros. has attitude—if you're looking for gluten-free options, you are most definitely in the wrong place.

Primanti Bros.' doors are always open.

The all-in-one concept is what makes Primanti Bros.' sandwich unique. It just doesn't seem natural to put the fries ON your sandwich, but the combination of that with the slaw, cheese, and tomatoes is one of a kind. There is no mayo in the cole-slaw; it is actually vinegar based. And don't try to mess with the combo; that insults the restaurant's intelligence. You get to choose your meat, and that is a more-than-generous offer.

Many cities are identified by their unique fast food places, and that's certainly the case here. Pittsburgh *is* Primanti Bros.

ESTABLISHED	1996	SPECIALTY ITEMS	SECRET MENU ITEMS
FOUNDER	Todd Graves	The Box	
GAME CHANGER	Chicken Fingers	The 3 Finger	
FIRST LOCATION	Baton Rouge, Louisiana	The Caniac	
TOTAL LOCATIONS	Over 225	The Sandwich	
TRADEMARK	The Box	Cane's Sauce	
		Texas Toast	
MASCOT	Cane II	**SEASONAL SPECIALS**	
CURRENT SLOGAN	ONE LOVE	Green Lemonade for	**BEST**
		Saint Patrick's Day	Fried Chicken (4)
CLASSIC SLOGAN	ONE LOVE	**MUST HAVE**	Ice (2)
		Chicken Fingers	
		Cane's Sauce	
		Texas Toast	

You Call That a Business Plan?

It was the early 1990s and Todd Graves wanted to open his very own chicken fingers restaurant. He and his original partner came up with a business plan in a course at LSU, and it got the worst grade in the class. Banks felt the same way about a chicken fingers fast food place, and would not give Todd a loan. But he believed in his plan, and worked as a boilermaker and Alaskan commercial salmon fisherman to raise

The first Raising Cane's, in Baton Rouge, Louisiana.

money for his idea. He managed to get a small-business loan and renovated an old building at the North Gates of Louisiana State University to create the first Raising Cane's. The restaurant is named after Todd's dog, Raising Cane, who serves as the proud sunglasses-wearing mascot (now Cane II after Cane I passed away). The first night the place stayed open until 3:30 a.m., and a chicken finger juggernaut was launched. So much for you, Professor, and those banks.

Since its inception, Raising Cane's has always been about keeping things simple. The food served is chicken fingers. The original menu consisted of three options—The Box, The Plate, or The Sandwich. The menu has since evolved into four choices, with The Caniac now being part of the mix. Fingers, fries, coleslaw, a side of Texas Toast (extra-thick brown bread), and a drink. That's it. And it's a formula that works.

This is who the place is named after.

Raising Cane's is rapidly expanding and can now be found in 18 states. It is a testament to Todd Graves finding something that works, sticking to it in spite of "expert" opinions, and continuing to do it well in many markets. There will always be a market for chicken fingers, and I bet that was part of the business plan that Todd submitted back at LSU.

One Love

Raising Cane's preaches "ONE LOVE," a love for chicken fingers meals and a tangible passion for them. Since day one, Todd Graves has preached and practiced this love, and his passion is contagious. In the fast food world, it's okay to be a one-trick pony as long as you do that one thing very well. Raising Cane's does.

The fingers aren't the only standout item at Raising Cane's. Homemade Cane's Sauce (its ingredients are secret) makes a big difference, and not just with the fingers, but the fries and toast as well. The fries are standard crinkle cut and the slaw is typical stuff. But the Texas Toast is grilled and always fresh, brushed with butter and garlic salt to make a perfect side item.

Taking a dip in Cane's Sauce.

These chicken fingers meals are quickly traveling north from Louisiana, and soon I believe you'll find a Raising Cane's in your neck of the woods if it hasn't already gotten there. Just look for the dog with the sunglasses and dig in.

SHAKE SHACK®

ESTABLISHED	2004	SPECIALTY ITEMS		SECRET MENU ITEMS
FOUNDER	Danny Meyer	ShackBurger		BurgerMeister
GAME CHANGER	A Hot Dog Cart in a Park	Shack-cago Dog		Cheese Dog
FIRST LOCATION	New York, New York	Shack Stack		Extra Shack Sauce
TOTAL LOCATIONS	Over 70	Shack Attack Concrete		Peanut Butter & Bacon
TRADEMARK	ShackBurger	ShackSauce		Burger
MASCOT				Shack-cago Burger
CURRENT SLOGAN		SEASONAL SPECIALS		Shandy
		Shack Corn Dog		BEST
		Many Frozen Custards		Burgers (4)—
CLASSIC SLOGAN	Stand for Something Good	MUST HAVE		*ShackBurger*
		ShackBurger		
		Black & White Cookie		
		Concrete		

Love Shack, Baby

Danny Meyer wanted to bring a roadside burger stand to New York City. In 2001 Madison Square Park was in disrepair, but the successful restaurateur's nearby establishments were thriving. So at an art exhibit in the park, a hot dog cart was rolled out stocked by one of his restaurants. After doing this annually for a few years, a park kiosk became available, and Danny grabbed a napkin and sketched out his

The "mother ship" in Madison Square Park.

idea—a modern roadside burger stand that became Shake Shack. Madison Square Park was the only Shake Shack location for five years, and the burgers and shakes at "the mother ship" were quickly hailed as the best in NYC.

Shake Shack's menu has always been simple. Burgers, hot dogs, fries, frozen custard, and drinks—that's it. There are many variations of these items (plus the ShackSauce), but the core remains the same at any Shake Shack you might encounter. The ShackBurger topped with lettuce, tomato, and ShackSauce is a staple, as are the many frozen custard Concretes that can be created.

The first Shake Shack was a New York City destination, and as the brand began to expand, it would carry this destination mentality along with it. Each of the new Shacks reflects the neighborhood where it was built (The National

The ShackBurger

Pastime Concrete is available at Nationals Park in D.C.). The menu is consistent in its basics, but there are variations depending upon the part of the world that you're in. It is very un–fast-food-like to expand at this slow rate, but Shake Shack is taking its sweet time to get things right as it stirs up a frenzy.

Shack Attack

My first trip to Madison Square Park was a memorable one. I had heard about this new great burger joint but couldn't fathom what it looked like. I was impressed by the online Shack Cam providing a live look at how long the line was. I saw a gap and decided to venture to the park to see what the big deal was.

An early lesson I learned at this Shack is that there are separate lines for drinks and food. I could order and eat my Black and White Cookie Concrete as I waited in the

A tasty Shack combination.

food line to order my ShackBurger. Once I tasted my custard, I understood what the fuss was all about. The burger confirmed it, but it is the overall feeling of the place that makes it special. Eating a burger, fries, and shake with others in a NYC park is a feeling like no other.

I like the crinkle-cut fries, but they remind me of my old Swanson frozen dinners. The Shack recently gave hand-cut fries a try, but switched back to the old crinkled favorites. I've been to many different Shacks since that first trip and enjoy seeing the menus mixed in with some local flavor.

ESTABLISHED	1949	SPECIALTY ITEMS	SECRET MENU ITEMS
FOUNDER	Nicholas Lambrinides	3-, 4-, or 5-Way Chili	
GAME CHANGER	Cincinnati Style Chili	Cheese Coney	
FIRST LOCATION	Cincinnati, Ohio	Skyline Dip	
TOTAL LOCATIONS	Over 130		
TRADEMARK	5-Way Chili		
MASCOT		SEASONAL SPECIALS	
CURRENT SLOGAN	Feeling Good, It's Skyline Time	Free Coney Day	**BEST**
			Chili (1)
CLASSIC SLOGAN	Whenever You're Feeling Good and Hungry It's Skyline Time	**MUST HAVE**	Hot Dogs—*Cheese Coney*
		Cheese Coney	
		5-Way	

Cincinnati Style

Nicholas Lambrinides cooked a lot of family recipes from his native Greece, and in 1949 on a hilltop overlooking Cincinnati, Ohio, he and his sons opened a small restaurant that featured one of his most unique—Skyline Chili. The family chili recipe is treated like the Colonel's original recipe in Ohio's neighboring state. The unique taste of the chili powers 3-Way, 4-Way, and 5-Way dishes and is the perfect topping for its famous Cheese Coney.

Skyline Chili is not chili con carne, the standard Texas chili that you're probably familiar with. Cincinnati-style chili is used as a sauce to pour over hot dogs, spaghetti, or whatever your hungry heart desires. Skyline has expanded into neighboring states and Florida and continues to grow, but no matter where the restaurant is located, the chili will always be known as Cincinnati style.

The most popular Skyline Chili item—Cheese Coneys.

Ways and Coneys

The Skyline menu is best known for two things that account for 75 percent of the restaurant's sales—Ways and Coneys. 3-Way chili is spaghetti topped with Skyline chili and cheese, 4-Way chili adds beans or onions, and 5-Way chili adds both beans and onions. You can mix other items into these "ways," but those are the standard combos. The other favorite is the Cheese Coney, which is a hot dog topped with Skyline chili, mustard, onions, and cheese. Skyline provides oyster crackers along with every meal.

My sports fanaticism is how I learned about Skyline Chili. As a Pittsburgh and Michigan fan, it is in my nature to strongly dislike any teams from Ohio. Many of these teams are sponsored by Skyline Chili. Naturally, I wanted to hate the product. But the first time I had some Skyline, I had to put my allegiances aside and enjoy the chili. A strong sampling of chili can do that to you.

ESTABLISHED	1962	SPECIALTY ITEMS	SECRET MENU ITEMS
FOUNDERS	Dan & Robin Foley	Sanchos	
GAME CHANGER	Taco Burger	Taco Burger	
FIRST LOCATION	Wichita, Kansas	Volcano Sauce	
TOTAL LOCATIONS	14	Refried Beans	
TRADEMARK	Sancho		
MASCOT		SEASONAL SPECIALS	
CURRENT SLOGAN	It's All About the Taste!		BEST
CLASSIC SLOGAN		MUST HAVE	
		Sancho	

Midwest Tex-Mex

Dan and Robin Foley brought tacos and nachos to Wichita, Kansas, when they opened their restaurant, Taco Tico, in 1962. The unique taste of Taco Tico beef was surprisingly sweet and unmatched, and after five years of success in Wichita it began to franchise throughout Kansas and neighboring states. Taco Tico's menu expanded as well, offering standard Tex-Mex cuisine plus Sanchos, which consist of meat, cheddar cheese, lettuce, tomato, and sauce in a large tortilla, and Taco Burgers, which is that same combo served on a hamburger bun. They also have four distinctive sauces—Mild, Medium, Hot, and Volcano.

The Foleys sold Taco Tico in the late 1980s, and the meat recipe was changed in an attempt to lower costs. Public outrage reversed this decision, but some damage was done. Taco Tico has also endured some financial problems that led to the closing of many locations, but the brand has begun to recover, keeping many Kansans filled with their Sanchos and Taco Burgers.

Kansas loves the Sancho!

A Taco Tico Fanatic–Richard Christy

Since I'm not in Kansas that often, I don't get to frequent Taco Tico as often as I'd like. So at this point, I will turn things over to my good friend and work buddy Richard Christy, a Taco Tico fanatic who grew up on this Mexican delight in his home state. Take it away, Richard . . .

My Love Letter to Taco Tico

Every fast food lover has one restaurant that they frequented as a child that brings back fond memories of family, food, and friendship every time they smell those sweet ingredients contained in their food. For me, it is the delectable Sancho from Taco Tico.

Sweet is a proper word to use for the Taco Tico Sancho, because there is some sort of secret ingredient that gives Taco Tico's ground beef a sweet and savory taste unlike any other Tex-Mex fast food restaurant. Their Taco Burgers, burritos, and taco salads all contain this delicious sweet ground beef that I grew up loving. My absolute favorite, though, is the Sancho. Basically a burrito with added vegetables, the Sancho was always my go-to. Especially on 99 Cent Sancho Day, which was like Christmas arriving early for me!

Richard Christy and I take our fast food and college basketball very seriously.

Taco Tico was the place my family visited every time something special happened in our life. I win a white ribbon in a 4-H skeet shooting competition? Let's go to Taco Tico! My sister wins a Leif Garrett autograph from our local radio station? Let's go to Taco Tico! As Taco Tico restaurants continue to disappear throughout the Midwest I fear that one day I will not be able to visit this Tex-Mex mecca to relive my great childhood memories, but for now, when I'm in Kansas my GPS is set to SANCHO!

—Richard Christy

ESTABLISHED	1928	SPECIALTY ITEMS		SECRET MENU ITEMS
FOUNDER	Frank Gordy	Naked Dog		Learn the lingo
GAME CHANGER	Hot Dogs and Yellow Jackets	Heavy Dog		
		F.O.		
FIRST LOCATION	Atlanta, Georgia	Strings		
TOTAL LOCATIONS	8	Ring One		
TRADEMARK	The World's Largest Drive-In	Fried Pie		
		Chili		
MASCOT		SEASONAL SPECIALS		
CURRENT SLOGAN				BEST
CLASSIC SLOGAN	What'll ya have?	MUST HAVE		Hot Dogs (3)
		Naked Dog		
		Ring One		
		F.O.		

What'll Ya Have?

In 1928 Georgia Tech dropout Frank Gordy opened a restaurant called Yellow Jacket heavily catering to Tech students. Later that year, using Yellow Jacket profits, Gordy opened a larger place down the block called The Varsity so the name would appeal to other campuses. By the 1950s The Varsity was the world's largest drive-in, with longtime carhops who would end up working there for fifty years. Customers came back not just for the food but also for the service, which always begins with someone asking "What'll ya have? What'll ya have? What'll ya have?"

Other locations opened in select cities across Georgia, starting in Athens, but the home base of The V never stopped growing. It currently accommodates over 800 people inside the store and 600 cars at the drive-in. This size is ideal for Georgia Tech football games happening right down the road across the North Avenue bridge. The menu offers all varieties of hot dogs and burgers; sides of chips, fries, and onion rings; chocolate or frozen orange shakes; and fried apple pie for dessert.

My naked dogs and strings walking.

Many well-known folks have eaten or worked at The V. Presidents Carter, Bush, Clinton, and Obama have stopped by. Nipsey Russell began his career as a charming carhop in the 1940s. Legendary employee Erby Walker worked at The V for fifty-five years moving people along, shouting, "Have your money out and food on your mind, and I'll get you to the game on time." The Varsity has always had its priorties right—great food and charming service that respects your timetable.

Naked Dogs Walking

You know you're in a special fast food place if it has its own lingo, and The Varsity has an extensive vocabulary you need to master to ensure your order is correct. A "hot dog" means a hot dog with chili and mustard. If you want a plain dog, that's a "naked dog," and if it's to go, that's a "naked dog walking." A "Mary Brown Steak" is a

Love those strings walking!

hamburger with no bun, and a "Glorified Steak" is a burger with mayo, lettuce, and tomato.

The lingo continues with any sides you might want to order. A "bag of rags" is a bag of potato chips, "ring one" is an order of onion rings, and "strings" are fries. As for drinks, there's a "P.C." for plain chocolate milk and an "N.I.P.C." if you want no ice in it. You can always settle for a "Joe-ree," which is a simple coffee with cream.

The orange drink at The V has lots of variations. A "Varsity Orange" is the standard drink, and there's an "N.I. Orange" if you don't want ice. A must-have is the "F.O.," which is a frosted orange drink—a frozen delight after you finish your dogs and strings.

ESTABLISHED	1988	SPECIALTY ITEMS	SECRET MENU ITEMS
FOUNDERS	Wing Lam, Eduardo Lee & Mingo Lee	Original Fish Taco	
		Banzai Burrito	
GAME CHANGER	Surfing & Fish	Maui Bowl	
FIRST LOCATION	Costa Mesa, California	Maui Onion Rings	
		Baja Rolls	
TOTAL LOCATIONS	Over 50		
TRADEMARK	Fish Taco		
MASCOT	Ono	SEASONAL SPECIALS	BEST
CURRENT SLOGAN		Tofu Banzai Bowl	Tacos (3)
		Lettuce Wrap Citrus Slaw Taco	Burritos (3)
			Fish (2)
CLASSIC SLOGAN	Drop In. Have Fun. Eat Well.	MUST HAVE	Uniforms (3)
		#2 Combo	

Surf and Turf

It's safe to say that Wing Lam and Ed and Mingo Lee were born to open a restaurant. The three brothers grew up in São Paulo, Brazil, spending quality time in their parents' Chinese restaurant and learning all about the business. They moved to California in the mid-1970s and would surf, often heading down to Mexico for better waves and a taste of the fish taco. In 1988 the brothers decided to bring the fish taco to California with their Brazilian and Asian influence, and Wahoo's Fish Taco was opened in Costa Mesa.

The menu hasn't changed all that much in over 25 years in the business. Fish, chicken, steak, and pork tacos are staples along with sandwiches and burritos. But the fish taco, which is in the company name, after all, is really what sets Wahoo's apart from other taco makers. You'll find wahoo or mahi-mahi inside the fish taco along with distinctive Brazilian or Asian spices. Coupled with sides like Maui Onion Rings, Taquitos, or Baja Rolls, a unique meal always awaits you at Wahoo's.

Wahoo's—catch that surfing vibe.

Surfing U.S.A.

The original Costa Mesa Wahoo's was located on a street surrounded by and inundated with surfing, and that vibe spilled over into Wahoo's decor. Surf stickers were slapped on the walls, and Wahoo's became the place for surfers to eat and identify with. The restaurant would actually schedule serving the food around the ocean tides. If the surfing was good, no food. If the tide was low, time to eat! Wahoo's was cool from the get-go.

A friend from California had told me about this place that makes great fish tacos and is a cool hangout. The cynical New Yorker in me had to see this for myself, so the next time I flew out west I dropped by and was very impressed. The staff knew I wasn't the typical surfer and I felt like a fish out of water, but the tacos and sides made everything all right.

Wahoo's will rapidly expand across the country regardless of whether or not there are waves. The portions are generous, the food is delicious, and wherever you are, you feel that you're on the Pacific coast as you down your tacos.

The fish taco—satisfying surfers, and more, for over 25 years.

WHATABURGER®

ESTABLISHED	1950	SPECIALTY ITEMS	SECRET MENU ITEMS
FOUNDER	Harmon Dobson	Whataburger	Bob Ranchero
GAME CHANGER	Five-Inch Bun	Whatachick'n Sandwich	Honey BBQ Chicken Strip
FIRST LOCATION	Corpus Christi, Texas	Whataburger Patty Melt	Sandwich
TOTAL LOCATIONS	Over 750	A.1. Thick & Hearty	Hulk
TRADEMARK	Orange Striped A-Frame	Burger	
		Spicy Ketchup	
MASCOT	WhatAGuy		
CURRENT SLOGAN	Just Like You Like It	SEASONAL SPECIALS	
		Avocado Bacon Burger	BEST
CLASSIC SLOGAN	We Build a Bigger, Better		Logos (5)
	Burger	MUST HAVE	OVERALL (4)
		A.1. Thick & Hearty	
		Burger	

What a Burger

Harmon Dobson was determined to serve a burger so big that it would take two hands to hold and so delicious that after taking a bite, customers would scream "What A Burger!" In 1950 that's precisely what he named his burger stand in Corpus Christi, Texas, and as he served big burgers on five-inch buns, the customers exclaimed the stand's name emphatically. Dobson capitalized on the instant success and quickly expanded into other markets, opening 17 restaurants scattered through Texas, Florida, and Tennessee by the end of the decade.

The 1960s introduced the memorable orange and white A-frame design that became synonymous with Whataburger. Dobson, a pilot, knew the design and colors couldn't be missed from land or air—tragically, he died in a plane

Whataburger location #1, in Corpus Christi, Texas.

crash in 1967. But Harmon Dobson's wife, Grace, continued to grow the company across the South through the next two decades, expanding the menu and introducing promotions like the Nickel Coffee Mug (a branded mug that still gets you refills for five cents!).

Whataburger has remained in the family for over 50 years, and its fresh product system limits its expansion across the South, from Arizona to Florida, to stay close to its food sources. Their focus on hospitality and emphasis on value continue to drive customers to the nearest A-frame again and again.

It's always been hard to miss a Whataburger.

Stickers and Sauces

Whataburger has always been about customizing your burger. There are very few secret menu items, because you can create any burger you want at the orange A-frame. In the 1990s simple, colorful round stickers were created to help communicate this customization, and Whataburger fans have since made them iconic. I

What. A. Burger.

still have my stickers from my first Whataburger order down in Texas.

Another go-to Whataburger item is its unique range of sauces. There's mustard and ketchup, but these range from Fancy to Spicy. You can put A.1., creamy pepper, or a host of other sauces on your burger, fries, or rings. The standard Whataburger is made with mustard, so make sure you specify what you want and confirm it with your stickers. Fresh, custom-made-to-order items will have you shouting "What A Burger!" with millions of other customers.

ESTABLISHED	1961	SPECIALTY ITEMS		SECRET MENU ITEMS
FOUNDER	John Galardi	Chili Cheese Dog		
GAME CHANGER	Specializing in Hot Dogs	Deluxe Dog		
FIRST LOCATION	Wilmington, California	Corn Dog		
		Junkyard Dog		
TOTAL LOCATIONS	Over 300			
TRADEMARK	The "W" logo			
MASCOT	The Delicious One (TDO)	SEASONAL SPECIALS		
CURRENT SLOGAN	World's Most Wanted	Chili Cheese Tamale		BEST
	Wiener	Sea Dog		Hot Dogs (4)
CLASSIC SLOGAN	Just Thinkin' About Those	MUST HAVE		Chili (2)
	Hot Dogs Makes Me	Chili Dog		
	Hungry	Chili Cheese Fries		

All About the Dogs

In 1961 John Galardi was a student at Pasadena Junior College looking to make a few bucks, so he started working for Glen Bell, the founder of Taco Bell. Galardi noticed the glut of SoCal burger, chicken, and taco places and wanted to open a hot dog stand. Bell's wife suggested the name Der Wienerschnitzel, which actually means nothing in German or English. Galardi thought the name was more memorable than John's Hot Dogs, and it stuck (or at least part of it did anyway).

One of the original Der Wienerschnitzel locations.

Sure, the name Der Wienerschnitzel stood out, but its products were a unique departure from California fast food—hot dogs and chili. The company quickly franchised throughout Southern California with its A-framed restaurants and 15-cent hot dogs. Other menu offerings included a Polish sausage sandwich and the chili cheese dog, which remains on the menu today. By the end of the decade there were 200 stores along the West Coast, and Der Wienerschnitzel was on its way to becoming the world's largest hot dog chain.

The 1970s brought about big changes, including adding burgers to the menu, the celebrated Saul Bass–designed "W" logo, and dropping the grammatically incorrect "Der" from the company name. Der Wiener Dog, the chain's mascot

Who doesn't love a good hot dog?

at the time, was stunned along with other loyal customers, but Wienerschnitzel was the future.

The next two decades saw tremendous growth, the addition of The Delicious One (America's most wanted hot dog), and the Wiener Wagon, a 40-foot food catering truck that shows up at almost every California event. Mini corn dogs, chili cheese fries, pastrami sandwiches, and other choices are now on the menu, but it's the classic chili and hot dogs that keep Wienerschnitzel on top of der game.

Remember the Der

Der Wiener Dog stayed with my brother and me for a long, long time.

I remember traveling to L.A. as a kid in the mid-1970s and seeing a TV ad featuring a cartoon dog talking about a hot dog restaurant called Der Wienerschnitzel. My younger brother and I thought it was the funniest-sounding name we ever heard, and although we didn't go to the restaurant during that trip, the name always stuck with me. Never underestimate the value of a name that stands out (or an animated talking dog).

Once I made my way to Wienerschnitzel (sadly after the Der was gone), I learned why it had become so popular. All variations of its hot dogs—original, corn, or chili— are inexpensive and scrumptious. Like Nathan's in Coney Island, Wienerschnitzel dogs have their own distinct taste, and you feel like you could eat twenty of them.

It was a risk changing the name of the brand, but Wienerschnitzel now celebrates the Der in its nostalgic advertising. And as long as the hot dogs don't change, you can call the place whatever you'd like.

JON HEIN'S ✳ BEST ✳ FAST FOOD —LISTS—

If a restaurant has been featured in this book, I consider it to be one of the best fast food places in the country. (Yes, you too, BK!)

It's impossible for one fast food restaurant to be the best at *everything,* although each of them strives to be just that. Some are better than others. That's just the way it is.

I have made a handful of global decisions to simplify these lists. I included a maximum of the five best places on each one, but sometimes I just had to supersize.

I did not distinguish between national chains and regional favorites. All fast food brands, big and small, have been pitted against one another. If you don't live near my best hot dog or burger, hop on a plane and make the trip—it will be worth your while. I know KFC aficionados who drove hundreds of miles across state lines to try a Double Down when it was first being tested in a few markets. I respect that kind of commitment.

So here are my lists, from burgers to fries, tacos to donuts, drive-thrus to logos, which culminate with my five best overall fast food places.

You might disagree with some of my assessments, and if so, feel free to sound off on Twitter at @jonhein or e-mail me at FastFoodManiac@gmail.com. I'm pretty sure that I'm right, but I am more than happy to be proven wrong.

Happy reading and eating!

Jon Hein's Best Fast Food Burgers

If I could display a "number served" count like the McDonald's signs once did, my total burgers consumed would probably read in the seven digits. Whether it's a slider, a Whopper, or a Royale with Cheese, there's nothing better than a tasty burger.

1. In-N-Out Burger—Double-Double

The legendary Double-Double

Simply the best. It's the only burger I have flown across the country to devour. I'm not a cheese guy, so I order the Double Meat, but the Double-Double is the legend. Two beef patties, two slices of American cheese, onion, lettuce, tomato, and spread (their secret sauce) on a toasted bun. Go my way, Animal Style, Protein Style, or whatever style you desire. It's always fresh. And always delicious.

2. Five Guys—Hamburger

"Two Patties!" are the magical words you hear upon ordering your burger at Five Guys. All burgers are made with two in-house-made patties and your choice of as many toppings as you like, ranging from ketchup and pickles to grilled onions and jalapeño peppers. Regardless of what you put on top, when that meat hits your toasted sesame seed bun and gets individually wrapped up in foil, a very special treat awaits you.

3. Wendy's—Dave's Hot 'N Juicy Double

Dave Thomas really knew what he was doing. His square, old fashioned hamburgers have always been the best tasting of the Big Three (McD's, BK, and Wendy's), and the Double is what I choose when visiting the place named for Dave's daughter.

The standard double features two square patties topped with two slices of American cheese, lettuce, mayo, onions, tomato, pickles, and ketchup (squirted in the shape of a W) tucked between two toasted buns. I go with the standard meat and pickles, and can never get enough of those squares.

4. Shake Shack—ShackBurger

Shake Shack is busy making its way across the globe, and the ShackBurger is the force behind it. The standard ShackBurger is a smashed patty topped with melted American cheese, lettuce, tomato, and ShackSauce surrounded by two Martin's Potato Rolls. I get a Double dry, and it tastes terrific. I don't even miss the pickles.

5. McDonald's—Double Quarter Pounder

The Big Mac is more famous, but it's the Quarter Pounder that keeps me coming back to the Golden Arches. Two quarter-pound beef patties topped with slivered onions, pickles, and ketchup on a sesame seed bun. I have ordered more number two combos than anyone else on this planet, and the DQP is the reason why.

Supersize Me!: Krazy Jim's Blimpy Burger—Quad

As a graduate of the University of Michigan in Ann Arbor, I must include the Quad from Krazy Jim's Blimpy Burger on this list. I lived on these burgers for four years, and they are truly one of a kind. Four small balls of meat are thrown on the grill, then you choose your roll, any grilled items, the type of cheese, and wet or dry condiments. My standard order was a Quad on a plain roll with grilled onions and pickles. Fresh and delicious every time from my favorite Ann Arbor dive.

Jon Hein's Best Fast Food French Fries

Shoestring. Waffle. Crinkle-cut. Thick-cut. Curly. No matter how you slice that potato, the ultimate fast food complement is the French fry. When they're hot, crispy, and the salt is just right, fries can make the meal.

1. Nathan's Famous

The crinkle cut. The red fry fork. The thickness. As good as Nathan's hot dogs might be, the fries are the lodestone that keeps customers coming back to Coney Island's finest. These fries are different from most. If you combine the perfect waffle fry and shoestring fry, this is what you end up with. Simply the best.

The best fries you'll ever have.

2. McDonald's

That red container with the arched *M* is irresistible. The fries are the perfect blend of salt and shoestring potato that makes it impossible to eat only one. Just thinking about these fries makes me crave them. Insist on getting these potatoes right when they come out of the fryer, piping hot . . . it makes all the difference in the world.

3. In-N-Out Burger

As an East Coaster, I lament my lack of access to In-N-Out fries. Whenever I fly out west, my first stop after leaving the airport is the closest In-N-Out Burger. Their thin shoestring fries are freshly cut in-store every day and cooked in vegetable oil. The key is using In-N-Out's secret menu to get these fries well done—that extra brown crispiness makes them even more delicious. If I lived out on the West Coast, these might move to the top of my list.

4. Chick-fil-A

Those cows keep telling us to eat more chicken, but what they fail to say is how good the waffle fries are at Chick-fil-A. These fries are freshly cut and crispy, and the surface area won't allow a drop of ketchup to spill through. The patterned potatoes provide a bigger, wider fast food fry experience and are the perfect accompaniment to a legendary chicken sandwich.

5. Five Guys

There's a reason the sign out front says Five Guys Burgers **and Fries**. A regular fry order is already enough for two, and *then* your bag gets topped off with additional fries from a handy rectangular metal container. Fantastic touch. Those moisture spots on your brown bag means that they're fresh. Don't close the bag! Letting the steam out makes them less greasy and just as tasty.

Jon Hein's Best Fast Food Milkshakes

Burger, fries, and shake—it is the fast food trifecta. It's my standard order whenever I try a new place, and a milkshake can make or break the meal. The shake must be thick, rich in taste, and make me dream about licking clean the metal cup they made it in.

1. Dairy Queen—Blizzard

It could be 11 in the morning or 11 at night. If I'm driving and see a sign for Dairy Queen, I will pull over to get an Oreo Blizzard. You can flip a Blizzard and nothing will drip out. It's that thick and delicious. It doesn't get any better than this DQ delight. Order one, flip it, and enjoy!

The DQ Blizzard

2. A&W—Root Beer Float

I know a float technically isn't a shake, but this tastes too good to not include. The only way to improve A&W Root Beer is by adding a scoop of vanilla ice cream to it. The root beer fizz naturally blends with the ice cream for a most memorable treat.

3. Chick-fil-A—Chocolate Shake

The chicken sandwich is the best, the waffle fries are great . . . and the chocolate shake is excellent. Chick-fil-A took years to make sure their shakes were just right before unleashing them. Not being able to suck it all up through your straw is always an excellent sign.

4. Steak 'n Shake—Vanilla Shake

I don't come here for the steak; I come for the vanilla shake. It sounds plain, but, boy, is it yummy. The Side by Sides and specialty shakes are interesting, but since 1934 Steak 'n Shake has been doing it right with their traditional milkshakes. Any burger/fry experience is completely lacking if you don't wash it down with one of these.

5. Wendy's—Frosty

Technically, the Frosty also isn't really a shake, but I had to include it on this list. At first the Frosty was only available in chocolate, but it actually had a bit of vanilla mixed in, since Dave Thomas felt 100 percent chocolate would overpower the meal. Vanilla fans got their own Frosty in 2006. You cannot use a straw with a Frosty. It is *that* thick . . . and that good.

Jon Hein's Best Fast Food Beverages

I've taken many fast food trips with drinks at the forefront of my mind. My standard is a Diet Coke or Diet Pepsi, but you can find those anywhere. When the ice plunks down into a non-dessert nonalcoholic beverage, these are my go-to's.

1. A&W—Root Beer

I still smile when I hear the jingle—"A&W Root Beer's got that frosty mug taste!" This franchise was founded in 1919 on its root beer. The special treat is made with cane sugar, herbs, bark, spices, and berries, then poured into a chilled frosty mug. It is simply delicious. It's the rare fast food place that I will visit for its beverage above anything else.

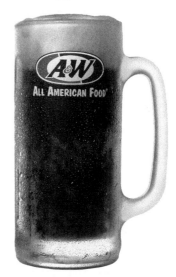

That frosty mug taste.

2. Sonic—Cherry Limeade

Sonic bills itself as being the Ultimate Drink Stop, and of the thousands of drinks you can conjure up, the Cherry Limeade is the must-have. The combination of fresh-squeezed lime and cherry sweetness is tangy and refreshing, and the best ice in America makes this drink last forever on a summer day.

3. Starbucks—Passion Tea Lemonade

I am not a coffee drinker, which kept me out of Starbucks for years. Then my daughters alerted me to the other drinks at Starbucks that are NOT coffee, and the best of the best is its Passion Tea Lemonade. This gem is composed of hibiscus and natural tropical flavors mixed with lemonade, and then hand-shaken by your favorite barista with ice. Keep the hibiscus coming.

4. Culver's—Root Beer

If you haven't been to Culver's, a Wisconsin-based restaurant chain, you're missing out on great frozen custard and delicious root beer. The proprietary Culver's Root Beer is made from a family recipe and comes right out of the fountain with a huge head and sweetness that lingers in a good way. Bring your own frosted glass to get the full effect.

5. Bojangles'—Legendary Iced Tea (sweetened)

Brewed fresh every day, the sweetened Legendary Iced Tea goes great with Bojangles' chicken and biscuits. Many try to make the perfect southern sweet iced tea, but Bojangles' has somehow nailed down this unique beverage. It's a must-have.

Jon Hein's Best Fast Food Fried Chicken

Any food that can be ordered by the bucket holds tremendous appeal for me. There are many different ways to fry a chicken, but the magic is always in the herbs and spices. Chicken is a fast food staple, and it takes a lot to make it finger lickin' good.

1. KFC (Original Recipe)

This debate starts and ends with the Colonel's 11 original herbs and spices. This original recipe cannot be topped. It is kept locked up in a safe at KFC headquarters for good reason. This chicken is just as good *cold* as it is piping hot right out of the fryer. Extra Crispy is for suckers—Original Recipe Kentucky Fried Chicken is as legendary as the man who invented it.

There's chicken. Then there's the Colonel.

2. Roy Rogers

The only chicken that comes close to rivaling the Colonel's is at Roy Rogers. Roy's originally offered roast beef, burgers, and a Fixin's Bar, but the chicken is what really made the place stand out. This chicken is so good that Hardee's acquired the recipe just to compete with KFC. It is a different blend of herbs and spices and a little bit crispier, but always worth a trip to Roy's for.

3. Popeyes

If you're looking for spicy fast food fried chicken, Popeyes is the place to go. This Cajun chicken competitor set itself apart with its Louisiana style and spicy taste. The Bonafide chicken is marinated for 12 hours and bursting with either spicy or mild Louisiana flavor. Yum.

4. Raising Cane's

Raising Cane's sells one main dish—chicken fingers. These aren't your typical fingers—they are high quality, always fresh, and never ever frozen after being marinated for 24 hours. You can taste the difference in the 100 percent chicken tenderloins, and since it's the only main dish on the menu, you know it has to be pretty special.

5. Bojangles'

Bojangles' offers the optimal complete chicken meal—its biscuits are excellent and its tea is so sweet. The chicken is very good, just not as good as the other places listed above. Its flavoring is spicy, but not as tangy as Popeyes, and the seasoning is rich, but not as good as Roy Rogers.

Jon Hein's Best Fast Food Hot Dogs

Some fans need a program when they go to a baseball game—I need two hot dogs. Coney, Chicago style, corn, or chili, these are my favorite fast food places to go to the dogs.

1. Nathan's Famous

This Coney Island great sets the standard when it comes to hot dogs. Ever since 1916 when Nathan Handwerker started selling the dogs based on his wife's recipe, they have tasted heads above the rest. I don't know what's in the hot dog and, frankly, I don't care: it tastes terrific and is deserv-

Nathan's—the best since 1916.

edly "world famous." Every Fourth of July we celebrate the birthday of the United States, and Nathan's celebrates the amount of hot dogs a human being can eat in ten minutes. God bless America.

2. Pink's

On the other coast, Pink's of Hollywood has been serving its hot dogs since 1939 and is famous in its own right. Tourists and locals line up every day for a taste of what the La Brea Avenue hot dog stand has to offer. The chili dog is the standout, but you can't go wrong with any Pink's combination. And you never know what celebs you'll run into at this official L.A. treasure.

3. The Varsity

What'll ya have? Those magic words have been asked since 1928 down in Atlanta, where they serve great-tasting dogs on steamed buns. The world's largest operating drive-in offers naked, chili, heavy, slaw, and other hot dog combinations, and they all are exceptional. Whether you walk a dog or stay right there, The Varsity is a can't-miss hot dog destination.

4. Wienerschnitzel

They lost the "Der," but Wienerschnitzel has never forgotten how to make a great-tasting hot dog. It's how this California mainstay has become the world's largest hot dog chain. The chili cheese dog has been a menu staple since the 1960s when the restaurant was called Der Wienerschnitzel, and is still its go-to dog today.

5. Sonic

You can order practically anything at Sonic, but their dogs sometimes get lost in the shuffle. Sonic has had Coneys on its menu since the 1950s and offers regional-style hot dogs of all types. The Footlong Quarter Pound Coney is plump, juicy, and actually a foot long, a perfect fit to devour in your car. That is how you Sonic.

Supersize Me!: Skyline Chili Cheese Coney

The must-have item in the Cincinnati area is the Cheese Coney from Skyline Chili. It is the most popular offering on the menu, with the chili, onions, and shredded cheddar cheese sitting right on top of the hot dog. I might not be an Ohio sports fan, but I respect the power and allure of this Coney.

Jon Hein's Best Fast Food Pizza

Fast food pizza is not New York or Chicago pizza. I love those styles best, but they're unavailable or not worth ordering in most of the country. The following restaurants offer a different breed of pizza—tasty in its own right and delivered to your door by the pie. That works for me. (I'm leaving the fifth slot blank out of respect for traditional pizza.)

1. Domino's

It's not just the delivery that keeps customers coming back. Domino's has been synonymous with fast food pizza for a very long time and is currently the world's largest pizza delivery chain. The cheese, sauce, and crust create

Domino's always delivers.

some kind of magical taste that makes eating an entire pie feel like you had just one slice.

2. Pizza Hut

Pizza Hut has been making pies since 1958 back in Wichita, Kansas. A lot has changed over the years, and the Hut's pizza has steadily improved. Offering a buffet in some restaurants certainly adds to the appeal, and any pizza place that puts hot dogs or pretzels in its crust ranks high on my list.

3. Little Caesars

I first encountered Little Caesars when I went to college, and it was hard to get past its delectable Crazy Bread. Once I got to the "pizza pizza," I was easily able to fill up on the two-for-one special. The Pan!Pan! has a saucier taste than its competitors that gets the job done.

4. Papa John's

Papa John's is what you would expect fast food pizza to taste like, and I mean that in a complimentary way. Its taste has improved over the years as the brand, and Papa John, seem to be showing up everywhere. It gets a bit tiresome seeing Papa John at every sporting event, as if a corporate spokesman was churning out the pizza. It felt better to support the little guy from Indiana.

Jon Hein's Best Fast Food Sandwiches

Bread, meat, toppings—it's so easy, right? Heck, I can create a decent sandwich, but the consistently best fast food sandwiches, subs, heros, or hoagies are unique conglomerations of fine ingredients, mouthwatering meats, and fresh bread. I'm hungry.

1. Chick-fil-A—Original Chicken Sandwich

There are so many sandwiches to choose from, but my top choice is a simple one. A chicken breast. A toasted, buttered bun. A dill pickle. That's all that goes into the Chick-fil-A Original Chicken Sandwich, but it's the best-tasting fast food sandwich I've ever come across. It was the first of its kind in 1963, and over 50 years later it's still the best.

The ultimate chicken sandwich.

2. Primanti Bros.—Almost Famous

The Yinzer in me wants to put this unique combo of a sandwich at number one, and it comes in at a very, very close second. The most economically packed sandwich from

Pittsburgh is composed of meat and cheese of your choice topped with French fries (in the sandwich), tomatoes, and coleslaw (in the sandwich) surrounded by two slices of fresh Italian bread. Your meal *is* the sandwich, and it is truly one of a kind.

3. Arby's—Roast Beef Classic

Arby's might not actually stand for "America's Roast Beef, Yes Sir" (a rumor I believed for years), but its classic roast beef sandwich has been filling up customers since 1964. There's something about their freshly sliced roast beef piled high on a toasted sesame seed bun. And that's without the Horsey Sauce!

4. Blimpie—BLIMPIE

The Hoboken founders of Blimpie wanted their "salad on a sandwich" to be as big as a blimp—and it's not a sub, it's a BLIMPIE. Your choice of fresh meat is layered with lettuce, tomatoes, onions, oil, vinegar, and spices stacked between two slices of fresh Italian bread. That's a BLIMPIE.

5. Subway—Italian B.M.T.

The all-time classic sandwich from Subway is the B.M.T. This Italian classic is filled with Genoa salami, pepperoni, and Black Forest ham and then stacked with lettuce, tomato, onions, and whatever else you desire, making it the Biggest. Meatiest. Tastiest.

Supersize Me!: Capriotti's—The Bobbie

I wouldn't be doing my job if I left The Bobbie off this list. This Delaware gem is made up of fresh homemade turkey, cranberry sauce, stuffing, and mayo surrounded by a hero roll. What sounds like a Thanksgiving leftovers meal is one of the best sandwiches in the country. Find a Capriotti's and give it a try.

Jon Hein's Best Fast Food Tacos

There are so many different types of tacos to inhale, and variety is exactly what I seek in these Mexican treats. If you build them, they will come . . . to my favorite taco places!

1. Taco Bell

Where living *más* starts—the Crunchy Taco.

This California giant always thinks outside the bun. Taco Bell is inexpensive, but that doesn't take away from its mouthwatering taco treats. There are so many options to choose from, but item numero uno on my list is the best-selling Crunchy Beef Taco. Make it Supreme and have a field day with other variations, but when it comes to Taco Bell, this is what *yo quiero.*

2. Qdoba

The company name is tough to spell, but its tacos are wonderful to taste. The ingredients always taste fresh at Qdoba, and they offer more options than most other Mexican food places. Qdoba has a different flavor from Taco Bell and Chipotle, with its five salsa choices and guac or queso, and it's out of this world.

3. Wahoo's

Fish tacos. Yup, fish tacos. And no one does it better than Wahoo's. The three brothers mix their Brazilian and Asian cooking style with a surfer attitude to create tacos with a different kick. Mix in cheese, lettuce, salsa, and their green sauce on your fish sandwiched inside a corn tortilla and indulge.

4. Jack in the Box

You might be surprised that the biggest-selling item at a burger chain is Two Tacos. Jack's Monster Taco is a large crunchy shell topped with American cheese, lettuce, and one-of-a-kind taco sauce. Simple, straightforward, and satisfying.

5. Chipotle

I'm a huge Chipotle fan (it's convenient that there's one in the building where I work), and I enjoy my meal of three soft tacos. I choose fresh chicken to be covered with mild salsa and lettuce, while others add cheese and sour cream to the mix. A solid, warm treat—times three!

Jon Hein's Best Fast Food Burritos

Everyone wants a burrito regardless of what time of the day it is. I love how the varied ingredients are neatly rolled up inside a delectable tortilla and waiting to explode in your mouth (or onto your shirt). Here's where you'll find my favorites:

1. El Pollo Loco

Here's a crazy chicken burrito.

It seems as if every fast food chain now offers a burrito, but the best has its origins from a chicken stand in Mexico. The Ranchero Burrito from El Pollo Loco captures the Mexican fire-grilled chicken sensation. It is chicken, beans, rice, cabbage, Jack cheese, cilantro, pico de gallo, and poblano cream sauce wrapped in a warm flour tortilla. That's some crazy chicken.

2. Chipotle

My work pal Steve Brandano introduced me to Chipotle's chicken fajita burrito, and I thank him on a weekly basis for this gesture. Chipotle takes a chicken fajita and wraps it all up in a large warm tortilla. The mix is just right, compact, and every bite has plenty of flavor. Delicious.

3. Wahoo's

I had heard of fish tacos, but never experienced a fish burrito until I went to Wahoo's. The Banzai Burrito is as wild as it sounds. Fish (or any protein Wahoo's offers) mixed in with Banzai Veggies, rice, beans, and green sauce. This combo makes for one of the most unique burritos you'll ever taste.

4. Taco Bell

It's not called Burrito Bell, but there are plenty of choices at Taco Bell. The king of them all is the XXL Grilled Stuft Burrito, which includes your choice of meat, cheese, rice, beans, sour cream, guac, avocado ranch, and pico de gallo wrapped in a warm tortilla. This is one mighty burrito.

5. Qdoba

The Mission-style burritos at Qdoba offer a ton of variety and tastiness. The cilantro-lime rice gives it a little spice with your choice of meat, beans, queso, one of its five salsas, and assorted veggies, lettuce, cheese, sour cream, and guac.

Jon Hein's Best Fast Food Fish

Fish often finishes behind burgers, chicken, and hot dogs when it comes to fast food priorities. But fast food fish is no afterthought, and you don't have to be a non–meat lover to sample some satisfying seafood. (Fast food seafood options are limited nationwide, so I've included only four on this list.)

1. Arthur Treacher's

As a kid, I absolutely craved this fried fish. There is a golden crustiness (and I mean that in the most pleasant way) that encases the flaky fish inside. This entire company was built on the across-the-pond concept of fish and chips, and Arthur

The best fish and chips you'll find in the U.S.A.

Treacher's provides something different in our drive-thru world. I still get the urge and immediately head over to pick up some of the best fish in fast food.

2. Wahoo's

Fish. It's the reason Wahoo's is quickly making its way across the United States. The Brazilian/Asian mix in its tacos, burritos, and other offerings highlights fabulous fish that you've got to taste. These surfers know their stuff.

3. Long John Silver's

There are really just two competitors in the fast food fish and chips market, and Long John Silver's is a formidable foe to Arthur Treacher's. The fish tastes similar, and if LJS is your only option in town, this pirate provides some goodness from the seas.

4. McDonald's

At one time it was the only non-meat sandwich option at the Golden Arches, and the Filet-O-Fish has been pleasing lots of customers over the years. The FoF is a fish patty topped with melted American cheese and tartar sauce and served on a soft steamed bun. It's a great option from the Arches if burgers or chicken just aren't your thing.

Jon Hein's Best Fast Food Ice Cream

We all scream for it. On a warm summer day (it could be ice-cold in January in my case), nothing tops a slightly melted scoop of ice cream. Except maybe sprinkles, or crunchies, or Oreos, or . . . here are the places that I'm heading to first.

1. Dairy Queen

I admit to having worshipped DQ since the early days of my childhood. That curl on top of a simple cone still does wonders for me. It's the best-tasting soft serve you'll ever find. Mix in the Blizzard and other DQ variations, and it's ice cream paradise for all of us. Whether I'm six or forty-six, I still feel the same joy when I pull into a DQ parking lot.

2. Baskin-Robbins

When it comes to "hard" ice cream, Baskin-Robbins is the place to beat. I was raised on its 31derful flavors and the best in-store chocolate chip ice cream that I have ever tasted. I worked at Baskin-Robbins in high school and never grew tired of tasting that flavor. *That* should tell you something.

Plain and simple. Delicious.

3. Ben & Jerry's

I discovered Ben & Jerry's in supermarket pints. Their ice cream is always about thick, plentiful chunks of your favorite topping getting mixed into a flavor. Chocolate Fudge Brownie still does wonders, and you've got to respect the earthy message that they preach. Make the pilgrimage to their Vermont factory and taste what this company is all about.

4. Carvel

Since I didn't have Dairy Queen when I moved out to Long Island, I discovered Tom Carvel and the joy of his soft-serve ice cream. Carvel offers Flying Saucers (ice cream between two chocolate wafer cookies), cakes like Fudgie the Whale and Cookie Puss, and chocolate crunchies that are better than sprinkles. A soft-serve vanilla/chocolate twist of Carvel with some crunchies mixed in is a most excellent ice cream treat.

5. Braum's

This midwestern ice cream comes straight from its own dairy herd, and you can absolutely taste the difference in its freshness. Over 110 variations of Braum's Premium Ice Cream are worth trying, from straight vanilla to Butter Brickle. You cannot re-create the farm freshness that makes Braum's ice cream taste so good.

Supersize Me!: Culver's

Anyone from Wisconsin would come after me if I didn't include the frozen custard offered by Culver's. Since Caramel Pecan in 1984, the calendar brings a new flavor of the day 365 days a year, and chances are if you've ever heard of a flavor, they will have it at Culver's. If you're traveling in the northern Midwest, this farm-fresh custard is worth a fast food stop.

Jon Hein's Best Fast Food Pastries

You can have these for breakfast or dessert, or sometimes for both meals, in my case. They're sweet and always a treat. It's tough to eat just one donut, roll, or muffin, especially when I pull into one of these places.

1. Krispy Kreme

When you walk into Krispy Kreme, you realize that you're in for something special. The entire operation is right in front of you to take in as fresh doughnuts take their ride under a glazed waterfall. Krispy Kreme doughnuts are light, sweet, and taste terrific. These are the best doughnuts that I have ever had. And if that HOT NOW sign is on, look out on the road, because I will be making that turn into glazed bliss.

Krispy Kreme bliss.

2. Dunkin' Donuts

A lot of us run on Dunkin' for its coffee, but this place would be nowhere without its delicious Donuts. Whether it's Munchkins or full-size Plain, Glazed, or Chocolate Kreme Filled, you can't overestimate the variety that Dunkin' Donuts offers. I'm partial to the Vanilla Kreme Filled donut, but you cannot go wrong with any choice from Dunkin'.

3. Cinnabon

It is virtually impossible to walk by a Cinnabon without being lured in by its aroma. Airport. Mall. It doesn't matter. I'll make the time for that scrumptious cinnamon roll once I catch its scent. And one Cinnabon roll with its delicious frosting lifts me into sweet gooey heaven.

4. Tim Hortons

This place up north knows its stuff when it comes to donuts. Its Apple Fritter and Dutchie are legendary, and the Boston Cream or any of the dips are nothing to sneeze at. Mix in the Timbits (think Munchkins), and you'll be thanking the late NHL defenseman for bringing such sweetness into your life.

5. Starbucks

Most go to Starbucks for the coffee, but there has to be something to eat with it, right? In addition to the many scones and muffins Starbucks offers, the old-fashioned glazed donut is pretty darn good and a perfect companion to the famous coffee.

Jon Hein's Best Fast Food Coffee

I encounter all different types of java as I travel across the country. Coffee is one of the hottest fast food trends these days, and nothing goes better with your favorite pastry than a cup o' joe from these fine establishments.

1. Starbucks

No real surprise here. No one does it better, and no one has had as much international coffee success as Starbucks. The brand has expanded over the years but never forgot what made it so famous. Regardless of the variation, it's nearly impossible to find a better cup of coffee on a more consistent basis than at Starbucks.

The leader and best.

2. Dunkin' Donuts

People are surprised to learn how much of Dunkin' Donuts sales are thanks to its coffee. The donuts are top-notch (number two on my Pastries list), but the coffee is what keeps many coming back for more. Perfect for sippin' or dunkin', a cup (or box) of joe from here keeps us all runnin'.

3. Tim Hortons

This Canadian giant continues to make headway with its warm cup of coffee. If Tim Hortons' coffee can keep folks north of the border warm and satisfied, it must be doing something right. A fresh cup of coffee is guaranteed every time regardless of how many pots must be dumped to get it right.

4. McDonald's

When McDonald's started to remodel its restaurants to accommodate the McCafé, you knew Ronald was getting serious about his coffee. And the Golden Arches have gotten this formula down with increased sales and satisfied drive-thru customers. It's hot (don't spill it!) and an excellent way to start your day.

5. Krispy Kreme

Look, they've got the best doughnuts, so let's cut Krispy Kreme some slack for its coffee. It's very good coffee, but not as good as that from the other restaurants on this list. Honestly, I'd rather they keep the focus on the doughnuts anyway.

Jon Hein's Best Fast Food Biscuits

I adore biscuits. Filling up on bread has never been a problem for me. I've gone to fast food chicken places just to order the biscuits. I mix and match burgers and biscuits at mall food courts.

1. Bojangles'

Bojangles' has top-five fast food chicken, and it definitely has the number one fast food biscuit. This buttermilk treat is pure bliss, so good that

Bojangles' biscuit is its own meal.

it is completely acceptable to order six of these beauties and bypass the chicken entirely. The biscuit is filling and tastes so good that you cannot have just one.

2. Popeyes

A close number two on the biscuit list, Popeyes could also sell its buttermilk beauties as the main event. This biscuit has the ideal combination of butter and fluff. It crumbles as you bite into it, a perfect chaser to your chicken meal. And Popeyes' biscuits rarely taste dry—they are a nice, warm treat.

3. Hardee's

These buttermilk biscuits are made from scratch and baked daily at Hardee's. And you can taste that difference. For breakfast, lunch, or dinner, this warm biscuit is not too soft and very filling. The biscuits have become one of the biggest selling points for Hardee's, and are well worth devouring.

4. KFC

Oh, the KFC biscuit. Selfishly, I was a fan of the soft rolls the Colonel once provided, but KFC joined the buttermilk biscuit game decades ago. The biscuits are good *if* you catch them at the right time. They harden quickly and crumble in your hands if you wait too long.

5. Church's

I'll give Church's credit for doing things differently, and its honey-butter biscuits are sweet when warm. Church's glazes its biscuits with sweet honey-butter, but the shape of the biscuit is smaller than the standard, and these sometimes come out harder than they should. This unique combo is worth sampling, though.

Jon Hein's Best Fast Food Chili

I find it hard to look at chili since it always appears to be a brown mess, but I don't have the same problem when it comes to eating it. This crazy combo can fill you up as a stand-alone meal or side, and will empty you out on its way down.

1. Skyline Chili

Certain food items become legendary, and their location also ends up sharing in the notoriety—like Coney Island, the birthplace of Nathan's. Well, when it comes to chili, Cincinnati, Ohio, is world renowned for its Skyline chili. This stop is worth making anytime you're in the state of Ohio. 3-Way, 4-Way, 5-Way, or on a Coney, the secret-recipe chili, which has been passed down for generations, is a must-have.

If you're in the Cincinnati area, go here.

2. Wienerschnitzel

Wienerschnitzel is known for its hot dogs, but the chili has also been there from the very beginning. Its chili cheese dog has been a menu staple and top seller since they started serving them (back with the Der) in 1961. Wienerschnitzel mixes up its beef, pork, powders, and pastes just right in its chili, which will have you coming back for more.

3. Krystal

Chili is a meal, a side, a topping . . . it's everywhere at Krystal. The beef is mixed with beans, seasonings, and spices that add some punch to your Krystal, Pup, or fries. It's better as a topping than on its own, and Krystal's must-have option is its Chili Cheese Fries (with a Ranch option to spice things up even more).

4. Sonic

It's no surprise that Sonic has a chili option among its many offerings. It's best on Sonic's Chili Cheese Coney, but you'll also find it on fries and Tots. (Once you taste Chili Cheese Tots, you'll never go back to just plain.) If the first three chilis on this list weren't so good, Sonic would be higher sheerly for its spiciness.

5. Wendy's

Wendy's is never afraid to offer menu items that the other fast food giants will not. Chili is one such option. Wendy's is the only place to get chili poured onto a baked potato in the fast food world. It's rich, meaty, and slow-cooked in the store for four hours every day. Pour it onto those sea-salted fries to add a little zip.

Jon Hein's Best Fast Food Ice

Ice, ice, baby. It matters. It really does. It can't dissolve too quickly. It can't get in the way of your beverage. And it needs to be allocated in the correct amount. Many people take fast food ice for granted, but not this cool customer.

1. Sonic

When it comes to frozen water, no restaurant approaches the ice that Sonic provides. Put it in a cooler and it will last for ages. It defies any heat in your beverage. I'm not sure what's in those little cubes, and I don't really care. There is a Facebook page dedicated to Sonic ice with over 200,000 likes. Try it. You'll like it.

The best fast food ice in the land.

2. Raising Cane's

There are those who can live on crushed ice alone (well, maybe not alone, but it's a heck of a diet), and Raising Cane's has some tasty little cubes. The ice mixes well with all beverages and also stands alone as its own, uh, meal.

3. Chick-fil-A

The chicken giant has developed a cultlike following, and its ice is yet another reason why Chick-fil-A is so beloved. Customers have ordered bags of the ice to go, and Chick-fil-A happily fills these requests. The ice holds the flavor of whatever you mix in with it quite well, and cows have no issue with us eating more of it.

4. McDonald's

This ice is solid . . . solid enough not to melt in your drink, but enough to provide a reminder of what you just had if you remain thirsty. It's a bit big and blocky, but their straws are so powerful that you barely even notice. No surprise that McDonald's gets the little things right.

5. Wendy's

This ice is big and thick like McDonald's and works best in larger-size drinks. It takes a while for the cubes to melt, which keeps your drink cold if a long haul is necessary. Wendy's ice holds up well and is good enough to crack this controversial top-five list.

Jon Hein's Best Fast Food Straws

Never underestimate the power of the straw. This cylindrical, oblong piece of plastic (never paper!) will make or break the taste of your shake. Color and presentation count, but sturdiness and size shine here!

1. McDonald's

One of the reasons McDonald's is so successful is that it does all of the little things right. The item that illustrates this best is the McDonald's straw. It is wider than most others. It is thicker than most others. And whether it's a soda, a shake, or even a McFlurry, this is the most powerful straw in the fast food universe. And it makes a world of difference.

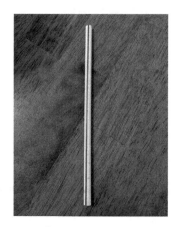

Thicker, wider, better.

2. Subway

Eat fresh . . . and drink with ease. The clear wrapping with the Subway logo is a nice touch as you unveil the white straw. It is easy to open and extremely durable. It's also the right length regardless of the size of your beverage.

3. Starbucks

It's no surprise that Starbucks straws are green to match the logo and look. With the number of beverages that Starbucks cranks out, it needs a straw that will not break easily. Mission accomplished. And two lengths of straws are available, depending upon your beverage size. Starbucks understands the straw needs of its customers.

4. Wendy's

The yellow and white straws at Wendy's have their work cut out for them with the Frosty on its menu. These straws are solid and almost unbreakable. You can use them with most beverages, but I wish you luck using any straw trying to suck down a Frosty. If the straw were a bit wider and stronger, it could move into the top three.

5. Hardee's

Hardee's offers a red straw that simply does not break. It is encased in your typical white paper covering, but opening it is a breeze. Whether it's a shake or a soda, Hardee's straw will flex as you need it to, but will not come apart. All that's missing is a little more width.

Jon Hein's Best Fast Food Secret Menus

Most fast food chains do not endorse secret menus (In-N-Out is a rare exception). I have partaken in this industry for a long time and discovered a variety of secret menu items through many resources. Unless otherwise noted, these secret menus are *my* discoveries, and not officially recognized by any restaurant. (See my full dossier beginning on page 261.)

1. In-N-Out Burger

The food is the best, but it is the secret menu that has made In-N-Out Burger legendary. The secret menu is the magic that lets customers know they are in for something special. From Animal Style to Well

In-N-Out's Not-So-Secret Menu

Done Fries, In-N-Out has the most extensive secret menu out there. I would chastise them for publishing their Not-So-Secret Menu on their website, but only a few items are up there. I am allowed to list secret menu items, but the restaurants can't. That's the first rule of Secret Menu Club.

2. Starbucks

Over the years many customers have created variations to their Starbucks coffee or tea order, and the Seattle giant was wise enough to incorporate these experiments into its menu. Extra shots of espresso change the color of your eyes, and Lord knows what you can do to a Frappuccino. Starbucks not only fills secret menu requests, it encourages them.

3. McDonald's

The sheer number of special orders made at McDonald's would dictate a secret menu, but the Arches do not embrace this notion as In-N-Out does. These rumored items come from longtime customers, and the staff may give you an odd look when you ask for a Land, Sea, and Air or the Mc10:35. But ask, and perhaps ye shall receive.

4. Taco Bell

As variety continues to spice up the menu at Taco Bell, the secret menu options have begun to grow as well. The Cheesy Gordita Crunch, which was an LTO (limited-time offer), was a popular secret menu hit. Now there are plenty of Quesa-options, and the menu continues to expand by the day.

5. Burger King

I had to include BK on at least one list, and they've earned their way onto this top five. Frings, the Rodeo Burger, and the Suicide Burger are solid secret menu options. Though if you're ordering anything at BK, you should probably keep it a secret.

Jon Hein's Best Fast Food Drive-Thrus

These windows and speaker boxes are critical when considering where to stop on the road. If the drive-thru doesn't run well, the quality of the food becomes irrelevant. It can be one of the most frustrating parts of your day, but not if you go to one of these restaurants.

1. Wendy's

One of the privileges I had as host of *Fast Food Mania* was a chance to work at the fastest drive-thru in the country—naturally it was Wendy's. From the moment you speak, there is a team on headsets dedicated to getting your order right and getting it to you quickly. Different people are assigned to tasks, and a coordinator pulls your order all together in a bag to go. It is a well-run machine, and why Wendy's has consistently been the top drive-thru in the country.

2. Chick-fil-A

Chick-fil-A offers the most accurate service and helped pioneer the double drive-thru. It looks nice—you'll always find a trash can in the drive-thru lane. That voice in the speaker is always friendly and makes sure your order is right. If you have a dog, many locations will have a treat at the ready. They keep things moving at Chick-fil-A.

3. Taco Bell

The second-fastest drive-thru in the nation belongs to Taco Bell. That's quite impressive considering the amount of variation one can put into a taco or burrito. Taco Bell puts an emphasis on customer interaction, focusing on the conversation as much as the food. It's a powerful combo.

4. McDonald's

The Golden Arches have been at this drive-thru game for a long time, and sheer volume is always a challenge. Almost every McDonald's now has an order confirmation board, which helps ensure accuracy. (I'm a big fan of these boards.)

5. Krystal

Krystal has been operating drive-thrus since the 1950s and knows how to make the most of any transaction. Krystal drive-thrus pride themselves on accuracy and use a ton of signage to make sure you know what to order. They could be a bit friendlier on the box, though.

Jon Hein's Best Fast Food Mascots

The face of the franchise. They tug at your heartstrings. They inspire you. They make you laugh. You dress up as them for Halloween. And ultimately, they bring you back time and time again to buy more of their company's fast food.

1. Ronald McDonald

Ronald

All of McDonald's legendary characters merit their own pages (Mayor McCheese would be tops, followed by Grimace and the Hamburglar), but the ultimate icon has to be Ronald McDonald. Ronald has always been the face of McDonald's, and kids can't get enough of this spokesclown. He's not very funny, but he's always smiling and bringing joy wherever he goes. He's instantly recognizable and synonymous with the Golden Arches' success.

2. The Colonel

Colonel Harland Sanders *is* KFC. His herbs and spices gave birth to the franchise, his salesmanship nurtured its growth, and his likeness is still on everything from boxes to billboards. An ad campaign featuring Darrell Hammond and then Norm MacDonald resurrected him 35 years after his death. That's staying power!

3. Cows

Eat. Mor. Chikin. The Chick-fil-A cows remind me how much I loved *Far Side* cartoons. What a great way to illustrate the strength of your brand. And the cows are all over Chick-fil-A restaurants as well as in its advertising, spreading the word.

4. Little Caesar

Little Caesars' mascot absolutely got me to eat their pizza. When I first saw a commercial, I walked around repeating "Pan!Pan!" over and over. Little Caesar (the mascot) with pizzas hanging off his spear gives the franchise its sense of humor and an unforgettable identity.

5. Rooty

Rooty was hibernating for a number of years, but the A&W folks wised up and brought back this lovable "root bear." Rooty is cute, funny, and lets everyone know about A&W's frosty mug taste.

Supersize Me!: The King

I cannot leave fast food royalty off this list, so I have to mention the ruler of Burger King. He has had several incarnations over the years, but the latest version with the mask freaks me out. I get the joke, but I also get how kids everywhere are terrified of that mask. Smart marketing.

Jon Hein's Best Fast Food Sweepstakes

As if the meal isn't already enough, you can also win some valuable prizes at your favorite fast food place. Cars (I've never seen it), cash (I saw this once), or more fast food (winner!). It's all in the game, yo.

1. McDonald's—Monopoly

I've been looking for Boardwalk and Pennsylvania Avenue since this sweepstakes first ran in 1987. Peel the tiny Monopoly pieces off the packaging of select food items and try to collect a set of properties to be a winner. Prizes include cash, cars, trips, more food, etc., but it's always about the food and always fun to play.

2. Tim Hortons—Roll Up the Rim to Win

If you're up in Canada in February, prepare to roll up the rim. Since 1986 anyone who rolls up the rim of their Tim Hortons coffee cup will see if they've won a prize ranging from Timbits, a car, a TV, or cash. The '80s contest created to help sell coffee in the spring has become an annual promotional bonanza for Timmy's.

3. KFC—Ultimate Family Reunion Sweepstakes

One lucky person wins a family reunion for up to 150 guests that includes KFC catering, four coach Amtrak tickets, a guest DJ, T-shirts, and banners. Buckets of the Colonel's chicken for 150 people? That is the ultimate family reunion.

4. Papa John's—Any Sporting Event

The Super Bowl. The Final Four. If there's a sports championship at stake, Papa John will be there and provide a chance for you to be there too. This proud Papa is so integrated into major sports that you expect to see him at these events, and his sweepstakes give you a chance to join him.

5. Subway—Subway Scrabble

I eat fresh often, but could never find an *A* playing the Subway Scrabble game. Scrabble game pieces were attached to sandwiches and drinks, then you went to their website to spin a wheel for an instant prize, and then tried to spell a word for other prizes. This took some effort, but then again, so does Scrabble.

Jon Hein's Best Fast Food Toy Collectibles

When my daughters were much younger, I made a rare appearance at Burger King for one reason—they had *Powerpuff Girls* toys. Collectibles are so popular at fast food places that you can skip the food and order *just the toy*. Superheroes. Glasses. Dinosaurs. Anything is better if there's a toy inside.

1. McDonald's

This toy fest started with the McDonaldland characters and has never let up. Whether it was a rubber band motorboat or tiny Play-Doh containers, toys were always awesome at the Arches. The Happy Meal begat Changeables, mini Barbies, Beanie Babies, Furbys, and Lord knows how many other licensed characters. Tip: If you're wondering what the next toy is going to be, look at the bottom of your Happy Meal box.

2. Burger King

When it comes to drinking glasses, BK cannot be beat. *E.T., Star Wars,* your favorite baseball team . . . all were available on the side of a glass. Burger King also had some great toys featuring the Teenage Mutant Ninja Turtles, *Jurassic Park, The Simpsons,* and Pokémon, but the cheesy BK Kids Club cannot be ignored. However, the old-school BK offerings are some of the best ever made.

3. Hardee's

Hardee's had a tough time keeping up with McDonald's and Wendy's, but that didn't stop them from creating plush Disney and Care Bears toys. Hardee's was *the* place for any California Raisins merch (who doesn't love those singing dried-up grapes?). The Cool Kids have been collecting at Hardee's since 2000, and with the licenses still in place, they will get their X-Men and more.

4. Wendy's

Peanuts. Wendy's capitalized on the popularity of Charlie Brown and crew in its Kids' Meal with toys that are sought after to this day. Wendy's has always been in the game with ALF, Furskins, *The Jetsons,* Snagglepuss, and Yogi Bear toys. Wendy's might not emphasize toys as McDonald's or Burger King does, but Superman and Wonder Woman are here with a host of other collectibles.

5. Taco Bell

Taco Bell said *"No más"* to toys and kids' meals in 2014, but that doesn't take anything away from how they played this game. I ran for the border to get my "Search for Spock" glasses, and when *Star Wars* returned in 1999 the best stuff was down at the border. Taco Bell offered vinyl Bellhedzes, Weird-Ohs, and talking Chihuahuas as surprise toys, so you never knew what could turn up in your Kid's Meal.

Jon Hein's Best Fast Food Logos

These pictures are worth a thousand words and more than a few pounds.

1. McDonald's

The Golden Arches. A fast food beacon to many, especially yours truly. Such a simple design but so effective. The moment you see that rounded *M,* you know exactly what you're in for. It brings a smile to your face. And some great fast food.

Instantly identifiable.

2. Krispy Kreme

Warm doughnuts are on the way.

I love the old-school feeling of the Krispy Kreme logo. It feels like something out of the 1950s with its red, green, and white coloring. But I also know that it means a hot, fresh glazed doughnut is coming. Now, that's the best of both worlds.

3. Starbucks

I'm not a coffee drinker, but you can't miss this beautiful logo. It has a maritime feel and seems to be everywhere, becoming the Kleenex of fast food logos. No words are necessary—you know you're at a Starbucks (the smell of the coffee is a dead giveaway too). That fishy smile is inviting you in for a drink.

Oh, that Siren smile.

No cows necessary.

4. Chick-fil-A

The chicken is in the *C*. The script is fun and playful. When you see this logo, you know a chicken sandwich will soon be on the way along with some waffle fries.

5. Whataburger

If you're down south, this orange and white *W* is impossible to miss. In the center is a tribute to the A-frame structure of Whataburger restaurants. The goal was to create a logo that would stop you in your tracks—and Whataburger succeeds. Give these guys a sticker.

Don't stare too long—you'll get dizzy.

Jon Hein's Best Fast Food Uniforms

The pirate hat of Captain Hook Fish and Chips employee Brad Hamilton from *Fast Times at Ridgemont High* attests to the importance of a fast food uniform. It's easy to make a Worst Uniforms list, but I'm all about positivity, so here are some of the best.

1. Sonic

Red, blue, and roller skates—that's a tough combination to beat. Everything about this drive-in is upbeat, including its uniforms. It's hard enough to balance an order as you're skating it out to a car, but these unis help you look good doing it.

2. Chipotle

I'm admittedly a T-shirts and jeans guy, and I feel people do their best work when they're comfortable. At Chipotle it's all about black T-shirts with restaurant slogans in white type on the back, ranging from their slogan "Food with Integrity" to "Sometimes Being Put Out to Pasture Is a Good Thing." Bravo!

3. Wahoo's

Everything about Wahoo's is cool, and the staff uniforms are no exception. The fish taco giant partnered with a skating brand to create stylish black T-shirts you'd see on the streets. Those surfers know a thing or two about marketing.

4. In-N-Out Burger

The white hat. The red apron. The uniform uniformity. Sure, it's old-school, but for whatever reason, it works at In-N-Out. Part of me sincerely feels that the food would not be as fresh if the uniforms were any different. Let me go put my paper hat on.

5. Starbucks

Starbucks pays attention to every detail, including its barista uniforms. The staff needs to look stylish and well put together, but comfortable enough to make lots of coffee. The fitted black T-shirt under the green apron is a classy corporate getup to look at as you spend your day at Starbucks.

Jon Hein's Best Fast Food Slogans

The right tagline can define a fast food brand for generations. This is ground zero in the battle over our fast food dollars. Countless gems of American pop culture have been created in the name of our fine cuisine. Don Draper would be proud.

1. "Where's the Beef?" (Wendy's)

If you were alive in 1984, you will never forget Clara Peller looking at burgers and asking her elderly friends a simple question—"Where's the beef?" This slogan became a catchphrase that captured the country's attention and never let go. It also made Wendy's part of a conversation that had previously been just between McDonald's and Burger King. Well done, Wendy's.

2. "You Deserve a Break Today" (McDonald's)

There are countless McDonald's slogans to choose from, but for me, the classic is "You deserve a break today." Upon hearing this, I automatically break into "So get up and get away to McDonald's" on pure impulse. Truer words have never been spoken.

3. "Eat Fresh" (Subway)

Subway is direct in everything it does. Its slogan reflects that personality. Yes, there are a ton of celebrity athlete endorsements, but ultimately when you get to the restaurant, two words stick out—Eat. Fresh.

4. "It's Finger Lickin' Good" (KFC)

Kentucky Fried Chicken has been known as KFC for a long time now, but when the portrait of the Colonel's face was on the bucket, the best way to describe the chicken was "finger lickin' good." That's precisely what the delicious fried chicken is, and the down-homeness of the phrase gave the poultry some attitude. Great, unforgettable slogan.

5. "Eat Mor Chikin" (Chick-fil-A)

The cows of Chick-fil-A have a simple misspelled message. It's exactly what cows everywhere and the folks at Chick-fil-A want us to do, and we are more than happy to oblige. Simple, direct, and funny—all that you need for a memorable fast food slogan.

Jon Hein's Best Fast Food Ad Campaigns

I remember looking forward to the next fast food ad that my favorite chain would come up with. I anticipated it like a new Rush album release or Nike sneaker design. And no matter where they went with the ads, these brands always got it right.

1. Taco Bell

A talking Chihuahua is only one of the many Taco Bell ads that keep us coming back for more. Think outside the bun. *Yo quiero* Taco Bell. Make a run for the border. The attitude of America's favorite taco place comes bursting through the TV on a daily basis. Fun brand. Fun food. Great ads.

2. Jack in the Box

Oh, Jack. Jack was the identity of Jack in the Box before the company unwisely decided to blow him up in a brand restructuring. Jack was wisely put back together and brought back in recent years. These ads have always had a snarky attitude and stay with you long after they air.

3. McDonald's

Used to be number one, but these ads have slipped dramatically over the past decade or so. The older commercials were works of art, keeping you coming back to the Golden Arches. Your favorite athletes playing one-on-one, a jingle that you couldn't get out of your head, a singing moon . . . all of these carved a place in pop culture. Wish I saw more of these types of ads these days.

4. Wendy's

No one will forget "Where's the Beef?" or company founder Dave Thomas finding himself in peculiar situations. These ads helped make Wendy's a major player in the hamburger wars. Since Dave passed away, Wendy's has turned its identity over to a Wendy of its own, but she lacks the impact of down-home Dave.

5. Subway

"Five . . . Five Dollar . . . Five Dollar Foot Long." That tune alone cements Subway's position on this list. I don't need another Olympic athlete telling me to eat fresh, but I sing along with that jingle every time it comes on my screen. Every time.

Jon Hein's Top Five Overall

I really do love them all, but here my five favorites.

1. McDonald's

If you've taken the time to read through all of these lists, you might have noticed how often the name *McDonald's* has come up. Whether it's the big things or the little things, McDonald's manages to get it done right. You can be in Walla Walla or Tallahassee and know what to expect from the Golden Arches. And it consistently delivers, which makes it my top pick for best overall chain.

In front of my favorite McD's on Route 110 in Melville, New York.

2. In-N-Out Burger

The only thing that keeps In-N-Out from the top spot is its inability to migrate to the East Coast (it's selfish, but this is my list). I understand the need to be near their processing facilities to guarantee freshness, yet somehow they've made it to Texas. In-N-Out has the best fast food in the land, so pack up the trucks and move up to number one!

3. Wendy's

Wendy's continues to improve every year. Its burgers and drive-thru have always been excellent, and I admire the attempt to improve the fries. As long as Wendy's continues to carry out the vision of founder Dave Thomas and adapt with the times, it will always be a strong contender for the top of my list.

4. Whataburger

Another excellent franchise that I wish would come to the Northeast. Whataburger has the tradition, the experience, and excellent customer service. The colorful round stickers on your wrapper represent how willing they are to customize your meal, and the food is an excellent fast food option. Bring those A-frames up north!

5. Chick-fil-A

The fast food franchise with the most potential is Chick-fil-A. It has a great chicken sandwich, tasty waffle fries, delicious shakes, and super-friendly customer service. The cows have become national icons, and the country is starting to eat more chicken. As Chick-fil-A moves into the Northeast, it will continue to climb up this chart.

TIPS AND TRICKS
(for any fast food restaurant)

No one likes to wait in line at any fast food place. It can be at the drive-thru. It can be inside. It doesn't matter—nobody likes to wait.

It might come as a surprise that most delays are caused by inexperienced customers. The staff at your favorite quick service restaurant have been trained and know what they are doing. Yes, sometimes the speaker at the drive-thru is broken, or maybe someone is at the end of his or her shift, but in my experience I've found many delays are due to a lack of training *the customer* when it comes to ordering a meal.

So here's a fast food customer user guide based on the wisdom I've gathered in countless visits to various establishments all over the globe. If everyone plays by these rules, our world will be a happier place.

Inside the Restaurant

You've made the decision to park your vehicle and enjoy your meal inside. You found a good parking space, and you stroll in all set to order your food. This is where our training begins.

Choosing the Correct Line

Typically there are multiple service lines for you to select from when you're ready to place your order, but the shortest line isn't always the right one to choose. Look carefully to see who is at the register. Search for a manager, who will be wearing a different-color shirt from the rest of the staff. This is the line you want to be on. If you see two people working one register, avoid it at all costs. That's usually someone training a new worker. Wait for them to be on their own. There is no strength in register numbers.

As you wait in line, look at the menu board above and prepare your order. It's unfair to save this task until you approach the register. Keep things moving and know what you want from the get-go. And when you're ordering, be specific. This is your order, which you can customize any way you would like to.

Once you pay for your order, do not move. Do not step aside. Do not let them take the next person's order. They should be working on YOUR order, and standing there like a rock keeps the focus on you. I'm 6 feet 2 inches tall, so I can often obstruct whoever is behind me. If I happen to be behind you, since you've read this manifesto and clearly taken my guidelines to heart, I will wait patiently.

When you finally receive your order, once again it's time to stay put and be sure to check everything. You don't want to go to your seat and realize that you're missing fries or your food is cold. You can slide over slightly to allow the person behind you to order at this point, but don't leave the counter until you confirm that your order is correct and ready to inhale.

If you are presented with an empty cup instead of an already filled beverage, a golden opportunity awaits. Stroll over to the soda fountain and add as little ice as possible to your cup. The soda is already cold. Start filling up, pause for a well-earned sip, and then continue until your cup overflows with carbonated drink. Find the matching plastic lid and puncture your top accordingly. It helps when you need to identify who got the diet soda. Your tasty beverage now awaits you.

Heading over to the condiments area, you should already have in mind what you're going to need for your meal. Straws, napkins, and ketchup are a given. Don't take fifty-seven of each, just take what you need. Five napkins is safe—lap, face wipe, hand wipe, small spill, and courtesy (for others). As for ketchup packets, four should be plenty, and if you end up not using them all, be sure to return them to the pile. That's good fast food karma.

Now you know your order is correct, you're fully loaded with your condiments, and you can sit down, relax, and enjoy your meal.

The Drive-Thru

Managing the drive-thru has become an art form. There are many variables to calculate and you need a little luck on your side. If you follow these guidelines, it will maximize your odds of having a quick, enjoyable drive-thru experience.

My first general rule of thumb is to avoid combination restaurant drive-thrus. It's tough enough to get things right with one brand, and multiple brands lead to multiple errors. If it's at all possible, keep driving until you find a stand-alone drive-thru.

1. Take Notice

When you pull up to use any drive-thru, you must immediately take notice of what's in front of you. There are two key elements—the amount of cars *and* the types of cars that they are.

My drive-thru rule to live by:

> **If there are five in line, head inside.**
> **If there are four in line, it's drive-thru time.**

The caveat to this rule is in the details. Avoid, at all costs, the following:

- SUV or minivan—This means an order for four or five people and a distracted parent at the wheel. If I see two SUVs, I'm heading straight for the parking lot.
- Cell phones—It doesn't matter what type of car it is, if the person is holding a cell phone, it means they are distracted or taking an order for someone else.
- Any SUV driver holding a cell phone is an open invitation to go inside.

2. Handle the Box

Once you've decided to stay in line, the next step is handling the "box." The box is the intercom where you communicate with the fast food place.

Many restaurants now have a video screen that confirms your order as you go. Love those. But that shouldn't stop you from overenunciating your order. You might think you're being obnoxious, but you're actually helping the folks working inside.

You've had time to wait and a giant menu board to stare at, so know what you want when you pull up to the box. If you don't see what you want or have a question, ask up front because once you start talking, everyone working inside is listening on headsets and beginning to compile your order. Changing your mind means making them start over again, and that's unfair. Plus it causes delays.

3. Go in Order

Main dish first, side items second, drinks third, desserts last. If it's a combo meal, know the number and be specific on the details following the general order. Your meal will be assembled in this order, and you're making life easier for all parties involved. Once you're done with your order, make sure it gets repeated to confirm it, and know how much money you have to pay.

4. Get Your Money Ready

As you pull around, be sure to have your money ready when you approach the window. No one wants to watch you search for your cash. Have a reliable change spot in your car to pull from, or check under your mat on the driver's side or in the crack between your seat and the armrest. There's gold down there. Pay for your order and get your food.

5. Check Your Order

Do not move your car until you check your entire order. Yes, it will cause some traffic behind you, but the last thing you want to do is pull away with the wrong food. You will be honked at—ignore it. You are *saving* everyone time with your quality control check. Mistakes are made—missing straws, one less order of fries, the list goes on and on. Take an extra thirty seconds to make sure you got what you asked for.

6. Avoid the ZoD

You never want to pull up into the waiting area that's two car lengths in front of you—what I refer to as the Zone of Death. Parking in the ZoD forces you to wait for someone busy working inside to stop whatever they're doing and bring your order out to you, completely defeating the purpose of using the drive-thru. Avoid the Zone at all costs. If the employee politely asks you to pull up, you may politely decline. You didn't make the mistake—they did when filling your order. If you're in a sympathetic mood, roll into the ZoD and take the "fast" out of your fast food.

7. Be Prepared

It's good to keep some fast food extras on hand in case you miss something during your confirmation check. Maintain a stash of straws, napkins, ketchup packets, and other condiments in the car so you're never caught short.

8. Set the Table

If you're eating in your car as you drive to your next destination, here's how you should prepare for the trip. Use the ZoD as your setup area. Take the napkins out of your bag, unfold one, and place it across your lap. This prevents stray crumbs and unwanted stains. Unpack your sandwich and place it on the seat next to you. Open the sandwich box or unwrap the paper it came in, and use this for your ketchup or other condiments. If you have a dual cup holder, put your fries in one slot and your drink in the other. Place the remaining napkins next to your sandwich, and your bag is now empty, to be used for collecting trash. Drive away with full peace of mind and avoid potholes at all costs.

If you're parking and eating in your car, the bag your food comes in serves a dual purpose. After setting up as I describe above, take the bag and fold it flat across your lap instead of a napkin. This gives you industrial-strength protection against stains down there. Place your trash on the passenger's seat, and once you've finished eating just dump those lap crumbs onto a napkin, and use the bag for trash.

JON HEIN'S
SECRET MENU ITEM DOSSIER

I honestly can't believe I'm about to do this. I'm sharing with you a list of my treasured collection of secret menu items. I have gone through my lifetime of notes and, for the first time ever, put them all in one place for you to peruse and use.

Secret menu items are meant to be just that . . . *secret*. That's why the official position of practically every fast food restaurant I profile in this book is the following: "We do not have a secret menu available to guests." The rare exception is In-N-Out Burger's Not-So-Secret Menu, which you can find on its website. But let's make this official on behalf of all other fast food places that I've profiled in this book:

> My Secret Menu Item Dossier has been compiled from various websites, reports, and personal visits to the drive-thru. In no way did any fast food establishment provide me with, or acknowledge, any of these secret menu items or confirm their existence.

Disclaimer done.

Try all of the secret items listed. Not all fast food workers are up on these, so it's up to you to help educate them at work. Of course, there's no better feeling than ordering something out of the ordinary and having the person at the register treating it like another day at the office.

And if I've forgotten any items, write to me at FastFoodManiac@gmail.com or tweet me at @jonhein. I will post it accordingly (and secretly).

Enjoy, and shhhh.

A&W

- **Firecracker Burger**—Red and green beer-battered Jalapeño Bottle Caps and spicy southwestern sauce added to lettuce, tomato, onion, two slices of American cheese, and two patties in a sesame seed bun
- **Mozza Burger**—Mozzarella cheese and Mozza sauce on top of bacon, lettuce, tomato, A&W seasoning, and a beef patty in a sesame seed bun

ARBY'S

- **Chicken Cordon Bleu sandwich**—Chicken breast with a piece of ham and melted Swiss cheese and mayo on a toasted sesame seed bun
- **Meat Mountain**—Chicken tenders, roast turkey, ham, Swiss cheese, corned beef, brisket, Angus steak, cheddar cheese, roast beef, and bacon
- **The Mike**—A large roast beef sandwich with one slice of cheddar cheese
- **Wet Fries**—French fries smothered in cheese sauce

BASKIN-ROBBINS

- **Donut Sundae**—Baskin-Robbins ice cream sundae on top of a Dunkin' Donut

BLIMPIE

- **The Blimpie Way**—Adding tomato, lettuce, onions, vinegar, olive oil, and oregano to any sandwich
- **Cheese Trio**—No meat, just three types of cheese on Blimpie bread

BURGER KING

- **BK BLT**—Bacon, lettuce, and tomato added to a regular burger
- **BK Ham and Cheese**—Ham and cheese with lettuce and tomato on a BK bun
- **Frings**—One half French fries, one half onion rings
- **Quad Stacker**—Four beef patties, four slices of American cheese, eight strips of bacon, and BK Stacker sauce on a sesame seed bun
- **Rodeo Burger**—Onion rings and BBQ sauce on a Whopper
- **Suicide Burger**—Four patties, four slices of cheese, bacon, and special sauce

BURGERVILLE

- **All Banana Milkshake**—Vanilla milkshake with fresh bananas mixed in
- **All Toppings Burger**—Self-explanatory
- **Protein Platter**—Your choice of meat with a side salad (no bread)

CARVEL

- **Mixed-In Crunchies**—Chocolate crunchies mixed into the middle of a chocolate/vanilla twist ice cream cup (thanks, Amy Kauffman!)

CHICK-FIL-A

- **Blueberry Cheesecake Milkshake**—Vanilla milkshake with a blueberry cheesecake mixed in
- **Dog Treat**—A small biscuit for your dog at the drive-thru
- **Free Icedream**—Exchange a kid's toy for a small ice cream cup instead
- **Fried Chicken Club**—Fried chicken (instead of grilled) on a club sandwich
- **Spicy Char**—Traditional chicken sandwich with spicy seasoning

CHIPOTLE

(Insists they have NO SECRET MENU ITEMS but will create any order)
- **Burritodilla**—A burrito with a grilled, crispy shell filled with cheese
- **Nachos**—Chips with melted cheese, beans, meat, and salsa
- **Quesadilla**—A burrito tortilla folded in half with your choice of filling
- **Quesarito**—A customized burrito wrapped in a cheese quesadilla

CULVER'S

- **Ultimate Grilled Cheese**—American and Swiss cheeses with tomatoes and mayo on grilled sourdough
- **Veggie Burger**—It's a veggie burger

DAIRY QUEEN

- **Banana Split Blizzard**—Everything that's in a banana split mixed into a Blizzard

- **Chocolate Chip Blizzard—**A vanilla Blizzard mixed with the chocolate used to dip DQ cones
- **Jack and Jill—**A hot fudge sundae topped with marshmallow

DEL TACO

- **Bun Taco—**A classic taco's filling in a hamburger bun
- **Go Bold—**Adding fries and secret sauce onto whatever you order
- **Stoner Burrito—**Half-pound bean and cheese burrito with red sauce, special sauce, and fries

DUNKIN' DONUTS

- **Turbo Hot Coffee—**An extra shot of espresso in your coffee

EL POLLO LOCO

- **Skinless Chicken—**Having the skin removed from the chicken

ELEVATION BURGER

- **BLT—**Bacon, lettuce, and tomato in between two toasted buns
- **Paleo Burger—**Two patties in a lettuce wrap with raw onion, jalapeños, tomatoes, and mustard
- **Thick and Rare Burger—**Two patties that are cooked rare

FATBURGER

- **Hypocrite—**A veggie burger topped with bacon

FIVE GUYS BURGERS AND FRIES

- **Cheese Fries—**Melted cheese added to an order of fries
- **Double Grilled Cheeseburger—**Melted cheese between two hamburger buns cooked twice for crispiness
- **Patty Melt—**A grilled cheese sandwich with hamburger patties (and toppings) added inside

HARDEE'S

- **The Harold**—Biscuits, gravy, eggs, and hash browns in a Styrofoam container (shredded cheese is optional)

IN-N-OUT BURGER

- **3 x 3**—Three patties, your choice of vegetables and sauce, and no cheese
- **4 x 4**—Four patties, four slices of cheese, vegetables, and a bun
- **Animal Style**—A patty smothered with lettuce, tomato, pickle, extra spread, and grilled onions. Fries too can be smothered with cheese, spread, grilled onions, and pickles.
- **Cheese Fries**—Self-explanatory
- **Double Meat**—Two patties (instead of just one) on the bun
- **Extra Large Shakes**—A bigger cup for your choice of shake
- **Extra Toast**—Extra cooking for a toasty hamburger bun
- **Flying Dutchman**—Two patties and two slices of cheese—that's all
- **Grilled Cheese**—Two slices of cheese, lettuce, tomato, and the bun
- **Neapolitan Shake**—Chocolate, vanilla, and strawberry mixed into one shake
- **Protein Style**—A lettuce wrap replaces your hamburger bun
- **Well Done Fries**—Extra cooking to ensure crispy, slightly burned fries

JACK IN THE BOX

- **Additional Ingredients**—As many patties or as much cheese or any other topping as you want (it's not free, though)
- **Ciabatta Bacon Cheeseburger**—A bacon cheeseburger on a ciabatta bun
- **Sourdough Buns**—Substitute a sourdough bun for sesame seed one

KFC

- **Mac and Cheese Bowl**—Mac and cheese inside a bowl with any additional toppings
- **Poutine**—French fries soaked in hot cheese and gravy

- **Side of Biscuits**—Adding biscuits as side items
- **Triple Down**—A third piece of chicken, more bacon, and cheese added to the Double Down

KRISPY KREME

- **Cup of Glaze**—Glaze poured right into a cup
- **Filled Doughnut Holes**—Doughnut holes filled with your choice of filling
- **Free Doughnut**—If the HOT NOW sign is on, you are entitled to a free Original Glazed doughnut to sample

KRYSTAL

- **Quad Cheese**—Four layers of meat and cheese

LITTLE CAESARS

- **Half and Half Pizza**—Half a pizza with one topping, half with another
- **No Cheese Pizza**—Self-explanatory
- **Stuffed Crust Pizza**—Order it just like Pizza Hut does it

LONG JOHN SILVER'S

- **Fried Crumbs**—Breaded remnants from the fried fish

MCDONALD'S

- **All American**—Normal-size hamburger with only pickles and ketchup
- **Chicken & Waffles**—McGriddle sandwich with chicken in the middle
- **Land, Sea, and Air**—A beef, chicken, and fish patty together on one bun
- **McLeprechaun**—A Shamrock Shake mixed with a chocolate shake
- **McKinley Mac**—A Big Mac with Quarter Pounder patties
- **Mc10:35**—A combination of the McDouble and the Egg McMuffin that was ordered at 10:35, when the changeover from breakfast to lunch happened
- **Neapolitan**—A vanilla, chocolate, and strawberry layered milkshake
- **Pie McFlurry**—A McDonald's pie blended into a McFlurry

PANERA BREAD

- **Power Breakfast Salads**—Egg bowls with turkey and steak
- **Power Chicken Hummus Bowl**—Chicken, hummus, spinach, cucumber, tomatoes, and onions in a bowl

PAPA JOHN'S

- **Cinnapie**—A baked pizza crust topped with cinnamon and brown sugar streusel topped with sugary icing

POPEYES

- **Deep Fried Apple Pie**—An apple pie that gets deep fried
- **Naked Chicken**—No breading on the chicken

SHAKE SHACK

- **BurgerMeister**—Cheeseburger topped with ShackSauce and ShackMeister Ale–marinated shallots
- **Cheese Dog**—Melted cheese on a split hot dog
- **Extra Shack Sauce**—Ask for it as a side item
- **Peanut Butter & Bacon Burger**—Bacon and peanut butter on a burger
- **Shack-cago Burger**—Relish, onion, cucumber, pickle, tomato, mustard, celery, salt, and pepper added to a cheeseburger
- **Shandy**—A mix of beer and lemonade

SONIC

- **Dr Pepper Orgasm**—Dr Pepper, lemonade, and Powerade
- **Frito Pie**—Fritos topped with chili and nacho cheese
- **Grilled Ham & Cheese**—Grilled cheese with ham layered in

STARBUCKS

- **Black Eye**—Two shots of espresso in a regular coffee
- **Cake Batter Frappuccino**—Vanilla Frappuccino with both vanilla bean and almond flavoring

- **Chocolate Dalmatian**—Java chips and chocolate chips added to a white chocolate mocha
- **Dirty Chai**—A shot of espresso added to a Chai Latte
- **Green Eye**—Three shots of espresso in a regular coffee
- **Raspberry Cheesecake**—White chocolate mocha with some shots of raspberry
- **Red Eye**—One shot of espresso in a regular coffee
- **Short Drink**—A tiny-size-cup drink
- **Thin Mint Frappuccino**—Tazo Green Frappuccino with chocolate syrup, mint syrup, java chips, and honey
- **Triple C's**—Cinnamon Dolce Latte, caramel syrup, and chocolate mocha syrup
- **Zebra Mocha**—Combination of white chocolate and chocolate mocha

SUBWAY

- **Old Cut**—A sub cut the "old way," digging a trench instead of slicing the bread
- **Pizza Sub**—Salami, pepperoni, tomato sauce, and cheese on your choice of bread

TACO BELL

- **Cheesarito**—Cheese with scallions and taco sauce in a soft tortilla shell
- **Double Grilled Quesadilla**—A quesadilla grilled twice for crispiness
- **Enchirito**—An enchilada stuffed with beef, beans, cheese, onions, and red sauce
- **The Hulk**—Guacamole added to a bean and cheese burrito
- **Quesarito**—A cheesy layer between two burrito shells with cilantro rice, your choice of meat, nacho cheese, and sour cream
- **Superman**—Cheesy double beef burrito stuffed with potatoes, sour cream, guacamole, and tortilla strips

TIM HORTONS

- **Chai Tea Hot Chocolate**—A chai tea bag in a regular hot chocolate
- **Toasted Sour Cream Donut**—A sour cream donut takes a dip in the toaster

WENDY'S

- **Barnyard**—Spicy chicken sandwich with ham, bacon, and beef separated by cheese
- **Big Bacon Classic**—A classic burger with bacon added to it
- **Meat Cube**—A four-patty burger (also known as the Grand Slam)

WHATABURGER

- **Bob Ranchero**—Breakfast on a bun with cheese, jalapeños, and picante sauce
- **Honey BBQ Chicken Strip Sandwich**—Honey BBQ sauce added to the chicken sandwich
- **Hulk**—A Powerade and Vault green soda mix

WHITE CASTLE

- **Bacon Crumbles**—A topping of thick-cut bacon crumbs
- **Harold and Kumar's Order**—Harold: 30 sliders, 5 French fries, 4 large Cherry Cokes; Kumar: same order, except Diet Cokes
- **Loaded Fries**—Fries smothered with bacon, ranch, and cheese sauce
- **Surf and Turf Slider**—Fish and beef sliders stacked on one bun

IN MEMORIAM

We fondly remember these fine fast food establishments that left us too soon . . .

Burger Chef—Born in Indianapolis in the 1950s and second only to McDonald's in locations for a time, the home of the Big Shef was eventually sold to Hardee's and closed in 1996.

Burger Queen—Queenie Bee was the spokesperson for this chain that became Druther's in the early 1980s and eventually converted to Dairy Queens.

Chicken George—This Baltimore-based fried chicken franchise founded in 1979 became the largest black-owned fast food company in the country until closing in 1991.

D'Lites—Nutrition-based fast food chain founded in Georgia in 1978 that expanded to over 100 stores before closing in 1987.

Dee's—You couldn't miss the Dee Burger Clown out in front of these Utah hamburger drive-ins, which were founded in 1932.

Gino's—The home of the Gino Giant (the first triple-decker hamburger) was founded in Baltimore in 1957 by two famous Baltimore Colts—Alan Ameche and Gino Marchetti.

Lum's—A chain of hot dog stands based in Florida that peaked at 400 locations and bought Caesars Palace in 1969 from its success.

Naugles—Southern California Mexican restaurant chain founded in 1970 by former Del Taco employee Dick Naugle that eventually merged with Del Taco in 1988.

Nedick's—A New York City landmark founded in 1913 that sold orange drinks, coffee, donuts, and hot dogs.

Pup 'N' Taco—Long Beach, California–based chain featuring tacos, hot dogs, pastrami sandwiches, and RC Cola that was bought by Taco Bell in the mid-1980s.

Red Barn—This barn-shaped restaurant chain founded in 1961 offered the Big Barney (think Big Mac), Barnbuster (think Quarter Pounder), and the first salad bar in 19 states before closing in 1986.

Steve's Ice Cream—Founded in Boston in 1973, the first ice cream store to freshly mix in Heath bars, M&M's, and more at the counter right in front of your eyes.

Wetson's—You would buy them by the bagful at this New York hamburger chain from 1959 to 1975, which was best known for its Big W burger.

Wuv's—A national burger chain from the late 1970s that was "fresh never frozen" and offered incredible fries and onion rings until it closed in the early 1980s.

ACKNOWLEDGMENTS

To my better half, Debbie, who is my special sauce that I love more than anything and the best In-N-Out on the planet.

To my daughters, Rachel and Emily, who couldn't make me prouder and are more wonderful than any Happy Meal.

To my dog, Molly, who rides shotgun through countless drive-thrus and always makes the staff smile.

To my mom and dad for having me and getting me started early; my brother Kevin and his family for their loving critiques and fandom; my in-laws Mel and Bette Ganz, who treat me like a son; Lauren, Marc, Jodi, and their families for their expertise and never-ending support; and to everyone in my family who has shared a meal with me, I say thank you.

To Gary Dell'Abate, who is the best on-air partner anyone could ever ask for and an even better friend.

To Howard Stern, who once ate like I did, for inspiring me every day to be better and creative. To Robin Quivers, who would never eat like this, for always giving her support and watching as much TV as I do. To Fred Norris, a quality guy who spends quality time with me during the breaks.

To J.D. Harmeyer and Steve Brandano, who helped me research this book on a daily basis. To Will Murray and Jason Kaplan, who never let me forget who I really am and make coming to work before the sun comes up an absolute pleasure.

To Richard Christy, Sal Governale, Ronnie Mund, Scott Salem, Nik Ruckert, Jim McClure, Ross Zapin, Benjy Bronk, Al Ragone, Ben Barto, Jon Lieberman, Shuli, Lisa G, Ralph Cirella, Lauren Muraczewski, Jeremy Coleman, Marci Turk, Tracey Millman, Teddy Kneutter, Tim Sabean, and all my pals at SiriusXM for helping me live the dream.

To Todd Anderman, Mark Seffinger, Peter Ginsburg, Frank Cernigliaro, Todd

Berlent, Brian Lava, Eric Pomerantz, Scott Rosenzweig, Jason Freeman, and Keith Banks, who have been dining with me since elementary school before we graduated to Luger's.

To Bruce Hartley, who can deconstruct a Subway lineup better than I can.

To the Kauffmans, Udells, Katzelnicks, Scharfs, and all my Melville friends for the many barbecues and trips to Carvel (and now Dairy Queen!).

To Meghan Smith and Rob Hobson for times I'll never forget on the road, Sharp Entertainment, Fay Yu, and the rest of the *Fast Food Mania* team for making a TV show I'm so proud of (and still full from).

To my agent Tony Burton, and my book agent Richard Abate, for making this dream of a book become a reality.

To Amanda Patten for her editing prowess, Jenni Zellner for her photo organization mastery, and everyone else at Three Rivers Press for their guidance and support.

I could not have completed this book without Greg Kirmser of Kirmser Photo Research, who tracked down the photos I simply couldn't land. Thanks as well to my college pal Craig Neuman and all friends of fastfoodmaniac@gmail.com for your out-of-town shots.

To the press and media contacts at all of the fast food restaurants I've profiled in this book for patiently working with me to make this as accurate as possible and dealing with my many e-mails and phone calls.

To all of my contacts at the many fast food restaurants I've included, thank you for being so generous with your time and your images. This book needed your photos, and you came through for me in a very big way. I sincerely appreciate it.

I sincerely thank each and every one of you for your inspiration and support.

PHOTO CREDITS

I would like to thank everyone who helped me take or track down all of the images that populate these pages. Getting these pictures RIGHT was one heck of a process, as my editors will attest to.

Thanks especially to my wife Debbie for enduring photo shoots at countless Long Island fast food establishments. It was all worth it, honey.

National Chains

A&W, pages 9, 10, 11, 217: Used with permission and are property of A&W Restaurants, Inc., 2015. **Arby's,** pages 12, 13, 14: Used with permission and are courtesy of Arby's Restaurant Group, Inc. **Arthur Treacher's,** page 15: Used for editorial purposes and falls within fair usage guidelines; page 228: Courtesy of Jeffrey via Creative Commons. **Baskin-Robbins,** pages 17, 18, 19: Used with permission and are courtesy of Baskin-Robbins. **Ben & Jerry's,** page 20: Used for editorial purposes and falls within fair usage guidelines; page 21 top: Courtesy of DVS via Creative Commons; page 21 bottom: Courtesy of Markus Tacker via Creative Commons. **Blimpie,** pages 23, 24, 25: Used with permission and are courtesy of Blimpie. **Bojangles',** pages 26, 27, 28, 234: Used with permission and are courtesy of Bojangles'. **Boston Market,** page 29: Used for editorial purposes and falls within fair usage guidelines; page 30: Courtesy of Mike Mozart via Creative Commons. **Burger King,** page 32: Used for editorial purposes and falls within fair usage guidelines; page 33 top: Courtesy of Mike Mozart via Creative Commons. **Checkers,** page 34: Used for editorial purposes and falls within fair usage guidelines; page 35 top: Courtesy of Andy Kobel via Creative Commons; page 35 bottom: Courtesy of Michele Gregerick. **Chick-fil-A,** pages 36, 249: Used for editorial purposes and falls within fair usage guidelines;

pages 37 bottom, 223: Courtesy of Cheryl Herman; page 38: Courtesy of Generic Brand Advertising. **Chipotle,** pages 39, 40, 41: Used with permission and are courtesy of Chipotle Mexican Grill, Inc. **Church's,** page 42: Used for editorial purposes and falls within fair usage guidelines; page 43: Courtesy of Nicholas Eckhart via Creative Commons; page 44: Courtesy of Scotty Spiegel. **Cinnabon,** page 45: Used for editorial purposes and falls within fair usage guidelines; page 46: Courtesy of Cheryl Herman. **Dairy Queen,** pages 47, 48 top: Used with permission and the property of Dairy Queen; DQ is a trademark of Am. D.Q. Corp and used with permission. **Domino's,** pages 50, 51 bottom: Used with permission and are the property of Domino's Pizza; pages 52, 222: Courtesy of Femme Run via Creative Commons. **Dunkin' Donuts,** pages 53, 54 bottom: Used with permission and are the property of Dunkin' Donuts. **Fatburger,** page 56: Used with permission and is the property of Fatburger, Inc; page 57 top: Courtesy of Michael Fletcher. **Five Guys Burgers and Fries,** page 59: Used for editorial purposes and falls within fair usage guidelines; page 60 top: courtesy of Jamie "JD" Harmeyer. **Hardee's,** page 62: Used for editorial purposes and falls within fair usage guidelines; page 63 top: Courtesy of Ron Zack via Creative Commons; page 63 bottom: Courtesy of Laura C. McConnell; page 64: Courtesy of Megadem via Creative Commons. **Jack in the Box,** pages 65, 66, 67: Used with permission and are courtesy of Jack in the Box, Inc. **KFC,** page 68: Used for editorial purposes and falls within fair usage guidelines. **Krispy Kreme,** pages 71, 72, 248: Used with permission and are courtesy of Krispy Kreme Doughnut Corporation; page 73 top: Courtesy of Tim R. via Creative Commons. **Little Caesars,** pages 74, 75, 76: Used with permission and are courtesy of Little Caesar's. **Long John Silver's,** page 77: Used for editorial purposes and falls within fair usage guidelines; page 78 top: Courtesy of Jeffrey via Creative Commons; page 78 bottom: Courtesy of Craig Neuman. **McDonald's,** pages 80, 81, 82, 83, 243, 248: Used with permission and courtesy of McDonald's Corporation. **Nathan's Famous,** page 84: Used for editorial purposes and falls within fair usage guidelines; page 85 top: Courtesy of Joey Manley via Creative Commons; pages 86, 214: Yuichi Sakuraba via Creative Commons. **Panera Bread,** pages 87, 88, 89: Used with permission and are courtesy of Panera Bread. **Papa John's,** page 90: Used for editorial purposes and falls within fair usage guidelines; page 91: Courtesy of Paul Rivera FoodTograpiya via Creative Commons.

Pizza Hut, pages 92, 93 bottom: Used for editorial purposes and fall within fair usage guidelines; page 93 top: Courtesy of Mathew James. **Popeyes,** page 94: Used for editorial purposes and falls within fair usage guidelines. **Qdoba,** page 97: Used for editorial purposes and falls within fair usage guidelines; pages 98, 99: Courtesy of Drew Luthern, burrito enthusiast. **Quiznos,** page 100: Used for editorial purposes and falls within fair usage guidelines; page 101: Courtesy of XNateDougX via Creative Commons; page 102: Courtesy of Craig Neuman. **Roy Rogers,** page 103: Used for editorial purposes and falls within fair usage guidelines; pages 104, 105: Courtesy of Chad Wilson. **Sbarro,** pages 106, 107, 108: Used with permission and are courtesy of Sbarro, LLC. **Sonic,** page 109: Used for editorial purposes and falls within fair usage guidelines; pages 111, 237: Courtesy of Cheryl Herman. **Starbucks,** page 112: Used for editorial purposes and falls within fair usage guidelines; page 113: Courtesy of Emily Hein. **Steak 'n Shake,** pages 115, 116: The Steak 'n Shake logo is a registered trademark of Steak 'N Shake, LLC; images used with permission and are courtesy of Steak 'N Shake, LLC. **Subway,** pages 118, 119: Used with permission and are courtesy of Subway, a registered trademark of Doctor's Associates, Inc. **Taco Bell,** page 121: Used for editorial purposes and falls within fair usage guidelines; pages 122 top, 225: Courtesy of Cheryl Herman. **Tim Hortons,** page 124: Used for editorial purposes and falls within fair usage guidelines; page 125 top: Courtesy of Dov Joffe. **Wendy's,** page 127: Used for editorial purposes and falls within fair usage guidelines; page 128: Courtesy of the Everett Collection via Creative Commons; page 129: Courtesy of Cheryl Herman. **White Castle,** pages 130, 131, 132: The White Castle images and materials and the "White Castle®" mark are the exclusive property of White Castle Management Co. and are used under license. No use, reproduction, or distribution is allowed.

Regional Chains

All American Drive-In, page 135: Used for editorial purposes and falls within fair usage guidelines. **Braum's,** page 138: Used for editorial purposes and falls within fair usage guidelines; page 139: Courtesy of Olsen Williams. **Burgerville,** pages 140,

141, 142: Used with permission and are courtesy of ©Burgerville LLC. **Cafe Rio,** pages 143, 144, 145: Used with permission and are courtesy of Cafe Rio. **Capriotti's,** page 146, 147 bottom, 148: Used with permission and is courtesy of Capriotti's; page 147 top: courtesy of Mathew James. **Carl's Jr.,** page 149: Used for editorial purposes and falls within fair usage guidelines; page 151: Courtesy of Craig Neuman. **Carvel,** page 152: Used for editorial purposes and falls within fair usage guidelines; page 153: Courtesy of Sigckgc via Creative Commons. **Culver's,** pages 155, 156: Used with permission and are courtesy of Culver's. **Del Taco,** pages 157, 158, 159: Used with permission and are courtesy of Del Taco. **Dick's Drive-In,** page 160: Used for editorial purposes and falls within fair usage guidelines; page 162: Courtesy of Olsen Williams. **Duchess,** pages 163, 164, 165: Used with permission and are courtesy of Duchess. **El Pollo Loco,** pages 166, 167, 168, 226: Used with permission and are courtesy of El Pollo Loco. **Elevation Burger,** pages 169, 170 bottom: Used with permission and are courtesy of Elevation Burger. **In-N-Out Burger,** page 172: Used for editorial purposes and falls within fair usage guidelines; page 174: Courtesy of Minesweeper via Creative Commons; page 212: Courtesy of Eliot via Creative Commons; page 240: Courtesy of In-N-Out Burger. **Krazy Jim's Blimpy Burger,** pages 176, 177, and 178 top: Used with permission and are courtesy of Krazy Jim's Blimpy Burger. **Krystal,** page 179: Used for editorial purposes and falls within fair usage guidelines; page 180: Courtesy of Olsen Williams; page 181: Courtesy of Cheryl Herman. **Pink's,** pages 182, 183, 184: Used with permission and are courtesy of Pink's. **Primanti Bros.,** pages 185, 186: Used with permission and are courtesy of Primanti Bros; page 187: Courtesy of Tom Murphy VII via Creative Commons. **Raising Cane's,** pages 188, 189, 190: Used with permission and © Raising Cane's Chicken Fingers. **Shake Shack,** page 191: Used with permission and is courtesy of Shake Shack; page 192 top: ©Peter Mauss, Esto Photography, used with permission and is courtesy of Shake Shack; 192 bottom, 193: ©Evan Sung, used with permission and are courtesy of Shake Shack. **Skyline Chili,** pages 194, 235: Used with permission and are courtesy of Skyline Chili; page 195: Courtesy of Navin Rajagopalan via Creative Commons. **Taco Tico,** page 196: Used for editorial purposes and falls within fair usage guidelines; page 197: Courtesy of Chuck Herman via Creative Commons. **The Varsity,** page 199: Used with permission and is courtesy of The Varsity; page 201: Courtesy of Bob "Wolfie" Wolf. **Wahoo's Fish Taco,** pages 202, 203, 204: Used with permission and are courtesy of Wahoo's. **Whataburger,** pages 205, 206, 249: Used with permission and are courtesy of Whataburger; page 207: Courtesy of JonesDR77 via Creative Commons. **Wienerschnitzel,** pages 208, 209, 210: Used with permission and are courtesy of Wienerschnitzel.

All images not otherwise credited are courtesy of the author.